LIVING ABOVE THE LEVEL OF MEDIOCRITY

A COMMITMENT TO EXCELLENCE

BIBLE STUDY GUIDE

From the Bible-teaching ministry of

Charles R. Swindoll

INSIGHT FOR LIVING

Charles R. Swindoll is a graduate of Dallas Theological Seminary and has served in pastorates for more than twenty-four years, including churches in Texas, New England, and California. Since 1971 he has served as senior pastor of the First Evangelical Free Church of Fullerton, California. Chuck's radio program, "Insight for Living," began in 1979. In addition to his church and radio ministries, Chuck has written twenty-three books and numerous booklets on a variety of subjects.

Based on the outlines of Chuck's sermons, the study guide text is coauthored by Ken Gire, a graduate of Texas Christian University and Dallas Theological Seminary. The Living Insights are written by Bill Butterworth, a graduate of Florida Bible College, Dallas Theological Seminary, and Florida Atlantic University. Ken Gire is presently the director of educational products at Insight for Living, and Bill Butterworth is currently the director of counseling ministries.

Editor in Chief:	Cynthia Swindoll
Coauthor of Text:	Ken Gire
Author of Living Insights:	Bill Butterworth
Assistant Editor:	Karene Wells
Copy Manager:	Jac La Tour
Senior Copy Editor:	Jane Gillis
Copy Editor:	Glenda Schlahta
Director, Communications Division:	Carla Beck
Project Manager:	Nina Paris
Art Director:	Lonny Matsuda
Production Artist:	Donna Mayo
Typographer:	Bob Haskins
Cover Design:	Michael Standlee
Cover Photograph:	Art Wolfe/Wildlife PhotoBank
Print Production Manager:	Deedee Snyder

ISBN 0-8499-8293-6

Ordering Information

An album that contains twenty messages on ten cassettes and corresponds to this study guide may be purchased through the Sales Department of Insight for Living, Post Office Box 4444, Fullerton, California 92634. For ordering information and a current catalog, please write our office or call (714) 870-9161.

Canadian residents may obtain a catalog and ordering information through Insight for Living Ministries, Post Office Box 2510, Vancouver, British Columbia, Canada V6B 3W7, (604) 272-5811. Australian residents should direct their correspondence to Insight for Living Ministries, General Post Office Box 2823 EE, Melbourne, Victoria 3001. Other overseas residents should direct their correspondence to our Fullerton office.

If you wish to order by Visa or MasterCard, you are welcome to use our toll-free number, (800) 772-8888, Monday through Friday, between the hours of 8:30 A.M. and 4:00 P.M., Pacific time. This number may be used anywhere in the United States except Alaska, California, and Hawaii. Orders from these areas can be made by calling our general office number, (714) 870-9161. Orders from Canada can be made by calling (604) 272-5811.

Table of Contents

1. This message is not a part of the series but is compatible with it.

Living Above the Level of Mediocrity

The trackless path of an eagle in high flight never fails to seize our attention. "The way of an eagle in the sky" is one of those sights Solomon of old acclaimed as being "too wonderful for me" (Prov. 30:18–19). The soaring eagle represents healthy independence, unintimidated courage, strong confidence, and an almost invincible determination to be different from the majority. Everyone admires those eagle-like qualities.

God never planned for His people to become submerged in the slimy swamp of status quo existence. On the contrary, He is pleased to have us soar, living our lives far above the level of mediocrity. This does not mean that we shall always enjoy great success or be financially prosperous or continually healthy or free from the demands and difficulties of humanity. But it does mean that we can counteract the gravity pull of discouragement and defeat.

My sincere desire is that you will find an enormous boost of encouragement in these pages . . . that you will catch a glimpse of hope which results in a fresh commitment to excellence. There is no better way to live! As Isaac Disraeli once wrote, ". . . it is a wretched taste to be gratified with mediocrity when the excellent lies before us."

Chuck Swindoll

Putting Truth into Action

Knowledge apart from application falls short of God's desire for His children. Knowledge must result in change and growth. Consequently, we have constructed this Bible study guide with these purposes in mind: (1) to stimulate discovery, (2) to increase understanding, and (3) to encourage application.

At the end of each lesson is a section called ***Living Insights.*** *There you'll be given assistance in further Bible study, and you'll be encouraged to contemplate and apply the things you've learned. This is the place where the lesson is fitted with shoe leather for your walk through the varied experiences of life.*

It's our hope that you'll discover numerous ways to use this tool. Some useful avenues we suggest are personal meditation, joint discovery, and discussion with your spouse, family, work associates, friends, or neighbors. The study guide is also practical for Sunday school classes, Bible study groups, and, of course, as a study aid for the "Insight for Living" radio broadcast.

In order to derive the greatest benefit from this process, we suggest that you record your responses to the lessons in the space which has been provided for you. In view of the kinds of questions asked, your study guide may become a journal filled with your many discoveries and commitments. We anticipate that you will find yourself returning to it periodically for review and encouragement.

Ken Gire
Coauthor of Text

Bill Butterworth
Author of Living Insights

LIVING ABOVE THE LEVEL OF MEDIOCRITY

A COMMITMENT TO EXCELLENCE

It Starts in Your Mind
(Part One)
Ephesians 6:11–12; 2 Corinthians 2:11, 10:3–5

December 7, 1941. The island of Oahu, Hawaii. Sunrise: 6:26 A.M.

It was a picture-perfect, postcard morning. Light northeast trade winds played over the peaceful South Pacific harbor as an armada of cumulus clouds sailed proudly overhead. The U.S. sailors stationed there yawned and stretched to greet the lazy Sunday morning. This idyllic setting seemed the least likely place in all the earth for a war to start, but at five minutes till eight, the calm blanketing Pearl Harbor was slashed by the ruthless propellers of enemy warplanes.

In a carefully planned strategy, 190 Japanese planes from 6 aircraft carriers swooped down from the cloud cover, diving to make their attack in coordinated waves of strafing and bombing. Around the island 25 submarines waited to pick off survivors of the air attack, while several two-man subs infiltrated the harbor to finish off the crippled U.S. fleet.

When the enemy strike force returned to the carriers and the smoke of battle cleared, 2,113 navy men and marines were dead, another 987 wounded.

The enemy's strategy had been meticulously planned, carefully coordinated, and almost flawlessly executed. With a loss of twenty-nine planes, five miniature submarines, and sixty-four men, the Japanese had sunk four U.S. battleships, badly damaged three more, and wounded an eighth. They had also demolished two destroyers and blown the bow off a third while putting several other warships permanently or temporarily out of commission.

As a Christian, you wake up to a Pearl Harbor of your own every morning. But it doesn't take place on an island in the South Pacific. Your enemy sets his sights on a small harbor where your thoughts, beliefs, and attitudes are serenely docked, tied to their moorings, seemingly safe. On any day, Satan can launch a surprise attack that within minutes can torpedo your testimony, char your character, and sink your spiritual life.

1

I. The Schemes of Satan

The warning Peter gives us concerning Satan reveals something of the enemy's strategy.

> Be of sober spirit, be on the alert. Your adversary, the devil, prowls about like a roaring lion, seeking someone to devour. (1 Pet. 5:8)

Satan is both relentless and ruthless. He not only *prowls;* he also *devours.* Consequently, you should keep your eyes peeled to his wanderings and your ears perked to his roarings. Once he is sighted, you should brace yourself for an attack.

> Put on the full armor of God, that you may be able to stand firm against the schemes of the devil. (Eph. 6:11)

The word *schemes* in verse 11 is transliterated *methodeia* in the Greek. From this we get our word *method.* If the devil is our adversary as 1 Peter 5:8 says, it stands to reason he will attack us. If he will attack us, it further stands to reason that he will have a *plan* of attack—a scheme, a strategy. And his strategy is to get to your mind . . . to lull you into mediocrity . . . to blunt the edge of your thinking . . . to cloud your reasoning.

Screwtape Schemes Again

In what many consider his most famous work, *The Screwtape Letters,* C. S. Lewis created fictitious correspondence between an elderly devil, Screwtape, and his young nephew Wormwood. Screwtape's counsel to the eager Wormwood reveals something of the true schemes of Satan.

> You will say that these are very small sins; and doubtless, like all young tempters, you are anxious to be able to report spectacular wickedness. But do remember, the only thing that matters is the extent to which you separate the man from the Enemy. It does not matter how small the sins are provided that their cumulative effect is to edge the man away from the Light and out into the Nothing. Murder is no better than cards if cards can do the trick. Indeed the safest road to Hell is the gradual one—the gentle slope, soft underfoot, without sudden turnings, without milestones, without signposts.[1]

Is there something in your life that is distancing you from God—inching you away from the light? It may be something small. It may be something good—even *religious.* But if it's a wedge, it will put an empty space between you and the Lord.

---

1. C. S. Lewis, *The Screwtape Letters* (New York, N.Y.: The Macmillan Co., 1960), pp. 64–65.

With a bright ray of revelation, Paul pierces the clouds to show us where the battle is really fought.

> For our struggle is not against flesh and blood, but against the rulers, against the powers, against the world forces of this darkness, against the spiritual forces of wickedness in the heavenly places. (v. 12)

Whether between nations or neighbors, battles on earth are only muted shadows cast from a larger spiritual battlefield—the spiritual forces of wickedness in the heavenly places. The spiritual battle is our real struggle. That's where eternity is won or lost—not at the Battle of the Bulge or at Normandy or Pearl Harbor. However, because the spiritual battle is invisible and, therefore, often inconspicuous, we are sometimes ignorant of it altogether. In 2 Corinthians 2, Paul warns the church to forgive a repentant sinner and reaffirm their love for him "in order that no advantage be taken of us by Satan; for we are not *ignorant of his schemes*" (v. 11, emphasis added). This word *schemes* differs from the one used in Ephesians 6:11. Here it means "thought" or "mind."[2] To paraphrase, we could say that *we are not ignorant of the fact that Satan has his sights set on our minds.* Satan is a cunning strategist. He knows the truth of the proverb "as he *thinks* within himself, so he is" (Prov. 23:7a, emphasis added).

You Are What You Think

Essentially, we tend to be shaped by what our minds think about most often. If you always think about yourself, you'll probably become an egotist. If you think about material things all the time, you'll most likely become materialistic. If you dwell on your fears, doubtless you'll grow paranoid; if on others' wrongs, you'll become bitter. But imagine—just imagine—what would happen if your thoughts focused not on bitterness but on the *forgiveness* of Christ . . . not on your fears but on the *hope* you have in Christ . . . not on the selfish accumulation of things but on the *unselfishness* of the Savior . . . not on exalted thoughts of yourself but on His *lowliness.* May I lift the shade on your personal thoughts and take a peek? What clutters your cranium? Work? Worries? Why not have a garage sale and get rid of some of that junk—and rearrange your mental furniture around Jesus (Heb. 12:1–3)?

II. The Stronghold of the Mind

Because the battle raging around us is unseen, visual aids are necessary. In 2 Corinthians 10:3–5, Paul helps us see the real war by putting a transparency on our overhead projector.

---

2. The Greek word is *noēma.*

For though we walk in the flesh, we do not war according to the flesh, for the weapons of our warfare are not of the flesh, but divinely powerful for the destruction of fortresses. We are destroying speculations and every lofty thing raised up against the knowledge of God, and we are taking every thought captive to the obedience of Christ.

In this illustration, Paul compares the mind centered on the flesh to a fortress. Ancient cities were often constructed with a surrounding wall for protection against enemies and wild animals. Within the wall were towers that rose higher than the walls and overlooked the surrounding terrain. In the event of an enemy siege, military strategists would climb these "lofty" lookouts and shout orders to coordinate their ground soldiers in a defensive effort. For a city to be conquered, the offensive forces would have to penetrate the wall and take control of these towers by either killing or taking captive the men in them. Similarly, the mind is a fortress. We build walls to protect ourselves and erect towers to keep a lookout for enemy attacks. Calling the shots in the tower is a host of cunning, united, and determined strategists known as our thoughts. They take counsel together to determine our strategy and coordinate the deployment of troops. But before you crusade to conquer foreign citadels for the Lord, you must first plant His flag in your own fortress. Is every one of *your* thoughts captive to the obedience of Christ (v. 5)? Or do you have some that desert the troops and run amok through your mind? If you keep having to drag those willful thoughts back by the scruff of their necks, kicking and screaming, I'd like to suggest a strategy not only to keep them behind bars but also to reform them into law-abiding citizens.

III. The Strategy for Spiritual Victory

Since Satan schemes to storm the stronghold of our minds, we must forge a strategy on the anvil of God's Word to combat his attacks. David, a great military leader accustomed to poring over battle maps, provides us with a simple yet profound plan to win the battle for the mind.

Thy word I have treasured in my heart,
That I may not sin against Thee. (Ps. 119:11)

In the following lesson, we will equip you to mount a major counterattack against Satan by *memorizing, personalizing,* and *analyzing* the Word of God.

┌─ *Striking Back* ─────────────────────────────

Of the eighteen U.S. warships sunk or damaged at Pearl Harbor, thirteen were repaired to later launch a counterattack on the Japanese fleet. Of the six aircraft carriers from that

Japanese strike force, four were sunk 180 days later in the Battle of Midway, and only a single destroyer survived the war. The war ended 1,364 days after it started, in crushing defeat for those who started it. And it ended on the deck of a U.S. battleship—not in Pearl Harbor, but in Tokyo Bay. In the past, Satan may have made some devastating strikes on your mind. But like the Pacific fleet, those thoughts can not only be restored but also mobilized in a counteroffensive against the enemy. Treasure God's Word in your heart and, thought by thought, the battle for your mind will be won.

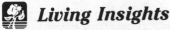 *Living Insights*

Study One

Second Corinthians 10:3–5 is a great passage to focus on. It contains the elements we need in order to strategically use our minds.

- The word choices in this passage are fascinating; studying them can be illuminating. Examine the meanings of the words and phrases listed here. Start with the immediate context; then expand to other Scriptures. Using a dictionary can give you added insight as well.

2 Corinthians 10:3–5

Word: *walk* (v. 3)

Meaning: _____

_____

Word: *flesh* (v. 3)

Meaning: _____

_____

Word: *war* (v. 3)

Meaning: _____

_____

Word: *weapons* (v. 4)

Meaning: _____

Continued on next page

Phrase: *divinely powerful* (v. 4)

Meaning: _____

_____

Word: *destruction* (v. 4)

Meaning: _____

_____

Word: *fortresses* (v. 4)

Meaning: _____

_____

Word: *speculations* (v. 5)

Meaning: _____

_____

Phrase: *lofty things* (v. 5)

Meaning: _____

_____

Phrase: *knowledge of God* (v. 5)

Meaning: _____

_____

Word: *captive* (v. 5)

Meaning: _____

_____

Phrase: *obedience of Christ* (v. 5)

Meaning: _____

_____

Living Insights

What a great way to begin a study guide! The battle for your mind is a fight that continually rages. This analogy is too rich to pass over lightly. Let's take some time to develop this battle scene in greater detail and in a more personal way.

- What are the battles in your mind? Certainly there are battles in your past, perhaps battles in your present, and most likely battles in your future. What follows is a page from your journal. Write an entry summarizing your thoughts on these battles. Talk about some of the successful strategies you have employed in the past. Write honestly and openly.

The Battles in My Mind

_____

_____

_____

_____

_____

_____

_____

_____

_____

_____

_____

_____

_____

_____

_____

_____

_____

It Starts in Your Mind
(Part Two)
2 Corinthians 10:3–5

Mediocrity germinates in the fallen Eden of the mind. There a labyrinth of thistles and thorns stretches over its surface, with choking vines reaching into every corner, touching every thought, every feeling, every attitude.

Every seed sown or dropped in the mind lies dormant, interred in its gray furrows. There those seeds of thought gestate silently, awaiting a springtime opportunity at new life. There they will sprout to full bloom and reproduce after their kind.

The mind is not fallow ground but fertile soil. If nurtured, it will bring forth orchards of fruit; if neglected, acres of frustration.

It is by the grace of God and the sweat of the brow that thoughts are brought captive to Christ. The sharp hoe of the Spirit can till the hardest of hearts and uproot the most stubborn of mental weeds. But that hoe must be held with hands that are both vigilant and diligent. For the garden is every inch a war zone, and the gardener must watch as well as work.

If we are ever to rise above mediocrity, we must first cultivate our minds. If we don't, they will become briar patches of tangled thoughts. Instead of becoming captive to Christ, our thoughts will run rampant, choking out anything good that has ever been planted. And Satan will claim the territory by virtue of squatter's rights.

I. The Schemes of Satan

As we begin a crop-dusting flight over our mental fields, let's take another look at the terrain we plowed in the previous lesson.

> Put on the full armor of God, that you may be able to stand firm against the schemes of the devil. For our struggle is not against flesh and blood, but against the rulers, against the powers, against the world forces of this darkness, against the spiritual forces of wickedness in the heavenly places. (Eph. 6:11–12)

Like an army of invading insects, Satan's ravenous horde is everywhere. His hierarchy ranges from kings to pawns, all dark pieces on the chessboard where he plots his every move with ruthless cunning. And his number one strategy is to keep God's kingdom in check.

> And even if our gospel is veiled, it is veiled to those who are perishing, in whose case the god of this world has blinded the minds of the unbelieving, that they might not see the light of the gospel of the glory of Christ, who is the image of God. (2 Cor. 4:3–4)

Jesus illustrates this scheme in the parable of the soils.

> "Listen to this! Behold, the sower went out to sow; and it came about that as he was sowing, some seed fell beside the road, and the birds came and ate it up." (Mark 4:3–4)

In verses 14–15, Jesus interprets this portion of the parable.

> "The sower sows the word. And these are the ones who are beside the road where the word is sown; and when they hear, immediately Satan comes and takes away the word which has been sown in them."

Satan blinds the minds of the lost concerning the truth of the salvation Jesus has to offer. In order to penetrate that spiritual darkness, the Holy Spirit must lift the scales off their spiritual eyesight. Satan's attacks are aimed primarily at the mind—a fortress under constant assault.

> For though we walk in the flesh, we do not war according to the flesh, for the weapons of our warfare are not of the flesh, but divinely powerful for the destruction of fortresses. We are destroying speculations and every lofty thing raised up against the knowledge of God, and we are taking every thought captive to the obedience of Christ. (2 Cor. 10:3–5)

To conquer a city in Paul's day, invaders had to find a way through the wall, storm the towers, and capture the commanding officers. This is Paul's frame of reference when he introduces the subject of spiritual warfare. For the carnal individual, the entire mind is a fortress that walls out God. In the event that the Spirit penetrates such a mind, Satan is quick to rebuild those carnal walls, to shore up the towers, and to provide a steady stream of sentries to rebuff the Spirit's offensive. It is the Spirit's job to conquer this carnal mind and bring it into subjection. Once God gains control over that rebel territory, Satan is forced to abdicate his position. But he knows the fortress so well that he is quick to launch a steady stream of counteroffensives. And he looks for any crack in the wall to gain an advantage.

Protecting the Mental Garden

Walls in the ancient Near East were used to protect not only cities but vineyards and gardens as well. Proverbs 24:30–34 describes the condition of one such vineyard.

> I passed by the field of the sluggard,
> And by the vineyard of the man lacking sense;
> And behold, it was completely overgrown with
>   thistles,
> Its surface was covered with nettles,
> And its stone wall was broken down.

9

> When I saw, I reflected upon it;
> I looked, and received instruction.
> "A little sleep, a little slumber,
> A little folding of the hands to rest,"
> Then your poverty will come as a robber,
> And your want like an armed man.
>
> What kind of shape is your mental vineyard in? Are there cracks in the walls where nocturnal rodents sneak in to steal away your fruit? Do you run off invading thoughts with a tenacious hoe, or are you a mental sluggard, laying back in your hammock catching forty winks? If the latter, don't be surprised to wake up one day and find your moral garden full of weeds.

II. The Seeds of Scripture

As every acorn contains a forest of oaks, so every seed of God's truth contains a potential orchard of spiritual fruit. If God's fruit is to triumph over Satan's weeds, His Word must be sown not only far and wide but deep as well. The best way to do that is to plant the Scriptures firmly in your mind.

A. Planting the Word. Romans 6:12–13 gives us our chores for the day's work ahead of us.

> Therefore do not let sin reign in your mortal body that you should obey its lusts, and do not go on presenting the members of your body to sin as instruments of unrighteousness; but present yourselves to God as those alive from the dead, and your members as instruments of righteousness to God.

Yet the nagging question is *how.* How do I yield myself to God? David frames a similar question in Psalm 119:9 and immediately provides the answer.

> How can a young man keep his way pure?
> By keeping it according to Thy word.

Still another question elbows its way through the crowd of theological issues: How can I keep God's Word? Where do I begin? Again, David hands our begging question a nourishing answer.

> Thy word I have treasured in my heart,
> That I may not sin against Thee. (v. 11)

As the harvest of a thousand bushels begins with a seed, so a life of righteousness begins with the right seeds planted early in life. Notice the emphasis in Proverbs on letting the seeds of wisdom your parents planted in your minds take root.

> When I was a son to my father,
> Tender and the only son in the sight of my mother,

Then he taught me and said to me,
"Let your heart hold fast my words;
Keep my commandments and live." (Prov. 4:3–4)
My son, keep my words,
And treasure my commandments within you.
Keep my commandments and live,
And my teaching as the apple of your eye.
Bind them on your fingers;
Write them on the tablet of your heart. (7:1–3)
Incline your ear and hear the words of the wise,
And apply your mind to my knowledge;
For it will be pleasant if you keep them within you,
That they may be ready on your lips. (22:17–18)

If we are to so treasure the words of our parents, how much more we should treasure the Word of God in our hearts and value it above all other advice.

An Almanac for Planting Scripture

To many, memorizing Scripture is like plowing without a mule, let alone a tractor. And that's a pretty tough row to hoe. If that's the case with you, here are some tips to help make it easier.

1. Choose a time and place where you can be free from distractions.
2. Set aside an adequate slice of time to tackle the task, say, fifteen to forty-five minutes.
3. Check the context carefully to make sure the verse should be applied to believers today.
4. Read the text out loud. Read it slowly, over and over, until you can repeat it confidently and without error.
5. Break the passage down into a natural cadence of phrases or thoughts in order to capture its rhythm.
6. Repeat the reference often to help orient yourself to the verse's biblical neighborhood. If you ever get a little turned around, it's always nice to have an address handy to help find your way home.
7. Underline the words or phrases you stumble over to help you walk securely through the passage.
8. Record in a notebook at the end of the day what you have learned from the passage and how the Lord has used it in your life.

B. Personalizing the Word. Substitute appropriate personal pronouns into the biblical text to make it more personal—for example: *I, me, my,* or *mine.* In John 3:16, for instance, you would say "God so loved *me*" as opposed to "God so loved the world."

C. Analyzing the Word. Use the passage you've memorized as a magnifying glass to analyze the Word as it relates to every area of your life. How does the verse affect your view of God? Of yourself? Your mate? Your children? Your friendships? What changes does the verse challenge you to make?

D. Harvesting the Word. Planting the Word in your heart, personalizing it, and analyzing it for application will enable you to reap bushels of benefits. It will help you gain control of your thought life. It will make you more alert to the needs of others and more sensitive to their circumstances. It will give your counsel the authoritative edge of truth that comes from God rather than man; as a result, your advice will be sought and esteemed. Your teaching skills will be sharpened; consequently, your effectiveness will increase. And, as a tangential benefit, so will your confidence.

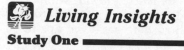 *Living Insights*

Study One

The message of this study is clear: If you expect to be victorious in your thought life, you must *memorize* God's Word. Let's look at a passage from the Psalms that underscores the value of taking the Scriptures seriously.

● Psalm 119 is the longest chapter in the Bible, as well as one of the most valuable. The theme of the entire psalm is the value of heeding God's Word. Read through this passage and list in the space provided the benefits of making the Bible a vital part of your life.

The Benefits of Obeying the Word of God

Verse: _____ Benefits: _____

_____

_____

Verse: _____ Benefits: _____

_____

_____

Verse: _____ Benefits: _____

_____

_____

Verse: _____ Benefits: _____

_____

_____

Verse: _____ Benefits: _____

_____

_____

Verse: _____ Benefits: _____

_____

_____

Verse: _____ Benefits: _____

_____

_____

Verse: _____ Benefits: _____

_____

_____

Living Insights

Study Two ▬▬▬▬▬▬▬▬▬▬▬▬▬▬▬▬▬▬▬▬▬▬▬▬▬▬▬

Satan feeds on the mind that is ignorant. He buffets the mind driven by emotion. But nothing fends him off like the Sword of the Spirit.

- Where are you in the discipline of Scripture memorization? For some, this lesson has served as an encouraging review. For others, it has been motivation to reestablish a slipping practice. And for still others, the concept of memorization is brand-new. Whichever category you fall into, strengthen the importance of Scripture memorization in your life. Carefully consider the eight tips suggested in this lesson and go for it!

It Involves His Kingdom
(Part One)
Romans 14:17, 1 Corinthians 4:20, Daniel 4:4–37

Ours is a world of secret codes. Not only do our nations speak different languages—here in this twentieth-century Babel, every profession speaks a different language as well.

Go to the doctor for a head cold; it's diagnosed as influenza. Philosophers postulate that the metaphysical realm exists as a conglomeration of monads. Lawyers consistently embalm the law with legalese. Even theologians and ministers shroud the truth in mystery. Like college students reading "See Spot run," they toss around such terms as *hermeneutics* and *homiletics* and *predestination* and *premillennialism* and *supralapsarianism*—words that have paralysis in their suffixed tails.

It's OK to not understand the in-house jargon of other microcosms in life. But when it comes to theology—the study of our God—we all need to use the same dictionary. One muddy theological term vital to our faith is the *kingdom* of God, for living by the precepts of this kingdom will lift us out of the me-first morass of mediocrity.

It's time to explain this term—this two-syllable enigma that's had us stymied for too long. It's time to define its mysterious colors in crisp, clear, black-and-white truth.

I. Understanding What the Kingdom Is
The New Testament helps us decode the term by giving us several kingdom characteristics.[1]
A. It isn't physical, but it is spiritual.
For the kingdom of God is not eating and drinking,
but righteousness and peace and joy in the Holy Spirit.
(Rom. 14:17)
It's not something you can physically touch or taste. But it is full of the Spirit's fruit to feast on (compare Ps. 34:8).
B. It isn't audible, but it is powerful.
For the kingdom of God does not consist in words,
but in power. (1 Cor. 4:20)
Like an electrical storm that displays its bright, white strength without a sound, the kingdom of God offers not words, but power.

---

1. The kingdom we're referring to here is not the physical messianic kingdom but "the kingdom of God in the spiritual sense in which it already exists in the souls of believers." Frederic Louis Godet, *Commentary on First Corinthians* (Grand Rapids, Mich.: Kregel Publications, 1977), p. 236. See also Philip E. Hughes, *A Commentary on the Epistle to the Hebrews* (Grand Rapids, Mich.: William B. Eerdmans Publishing Co., 1977), p. 559.

C. It isn't visible, but it is unshakable.

> Therefore, since we receive a kingdom which cannot be shaken, let us show gratitude, by which we may offer to God an acceptable service with reverence and awe. (Heb. 12:28)

This kingdom full of good things—joy, peace, righteousness, power, stability—is *given* to us by God (Matt. 6:33). Why does He deserve our gratitude, our reverence, our awe? Hebrews 12:29 answers, "For our God is a consuming fire."

D. An outline to remember. Here's a way to view the Bible and make the meaning of the kingdom stick forever in your mind.

1. God creates all things and establishes His authority over all (Gen. 1 and 2). From the plant kingdom to the animal kingdom to man, God's rule is intended to encompass all the kingdoms of the earth.

2. Man rebels against God's authority (Gen. 3). With the enemy's encouragement, man yells defiantly, "I will rule my own life. I will establish my own kingdom."

3. God moves through history to reestablish His authority (Gen. 4–Rev. 22). From the beginning of time, man has fought God for the throne. Still raising arms against His rule, we're in the heat of this battle today. The kingdom, then, is the invisible realm where God exercises His full authority over every part of us—over our hearts, our minds, our wills.

His Offer—Your Choice

> Psalm 103:19 nutshells the essence of the kingdom.
> The Lord has established His throne in the heavens;
> And His sovereignty rules over all.[2]

From Eden's brief innocence to today's permeating corruption, God's kingdom has remained intact. Amazingly, God still offers us His kingdom—even though we rebel against it. He is still eager to pour out righteousness and peace and joy . . . still eager to give power. Are you an empty vessel, ready to accept His control over your life and receive His good gifts? Or are you so filled to the rim with self that there's no room for even a drop of His sovereignty? He will not force you to pull out the stopper and drain your own authority. He longs to give you the kingdom—but the choice is entirely yours.

---

2. Rooted in the word *sovereignty* is the term *king* or *queen*. When used in this manner, it conveys the idea of kingdom authority.

II. Viewing the Kingdom through an Old Testament Example

Although the word *kingdom* is never mentioned in the story of Nebuchadnezzar, its message fills the pages of his biography. Nebuchadnezzar is one man who learned the hard way who belongs on the throne of our hearts.

A. The dream. One night King Nebuchadnezzar had a troubling dream, and he ordered all the wise men of Babylon to come before him to interpret it. But Daniel, the king's young Hebrew hostage, was the only one who could decode the nightmare. He told King Nebuchadnezzar:

> "The tree you saw, which became large and grew strong, whose height reached to the sky and was visible to all the earth, and whose foliage was beautiful and its fruit abundant, and in which was food for all, under which the beasts of the field dwelt and in whose branches the birds of the sky lodged—it is you, O king; for you have become great and grown strong, and your majesty has become great and reached to the sky and your dominion to the end of the earth. And in that the king saw an angelic watcher, a holy one, descending from heaven and saying, 'Chop down the tree and destroy it; yet leave the stump with its roots in the ground, but with a band of iron and bronze around it in the new grass of the field, and let him be drenched with the dew of heaven, and let him share with the beasts of the field until seven periods of time pass over him.'" (Dan. 4:20–23)

B. The interpretation. Daniel then hit him with the meaning:

> "This is the interpretation, O king, and this is the decree of the Most High, which has come upon my lord the king: that you be driven away from mankind, and your dwelling place be with the beasts of the field, and you be given grass to eat like cattle and be drenched with the dew of heaven; and seven periods of time will pass over you, until you recognize that the Most High is ruler over the realm of mankind, and bestows it on whomever He wishes. And in that it was commanded to leave the stump with the roots of the tree, your kingdom will be assured to you after you recognize that it is Heaven that rules. O king, may my advice be pleasing to you: break away now from your sins by doing righteousness, and from your

iniquities by showing mercy to the poor, in case there
may be a prolonging of your prosperity."[3] (vv. 24–27)

C. The king's haughty response. Do you think Nebuchadnezzar
heeded Daniel's plea for repentance? Not on your life.

> Twelve months later . . . the king reflected and said,
> "Is this not Babylon the great, which *I myself* have
> built as a royal residence by the might of *my* power
> and for the glory of *my* majesty?" (vv. 29–30, empha-
> sis added)

D. The fulfillment. Walking the palace's royal roof, King Nebuchadnezzar almost broke his arm patting himself on the back.
But look what happened next.

> "While the word was in the king's mouth, a voice came
> from heaven, saying, 'King Nebuchadnezzar, to you it
> is declared: sovereignty has been removed from you,
> and you will be driven away from mankind, and your
> dwelling place will be with the beasts of the field. You
> will be given grass to eat like cattle, and seven periods
> of time will pass over you, until you recognize that
> the Most High is ruler over the realm of mankind,
> and bestows it on whomever He wishes.' " (vv. 31–32)

This shuddering decree became reality just seconds after it was
made.

> "Immediately the word concerning Nebuchadnezzar
> was fulfilled; and he was driven away from mankind
> and began eating grass like cattle, and his body was
> drenched with the dew of heaven, until his hair had
> grown like eagles' feathers and his nails like birds'
> claws." (v. 33)

E. The king's humble response. Nebuchadnezzar's own sovereignty had been completely removed; his will, broken. A help-
less, dew-drenched beast, he now turned his eyes heavenward.

> "But at the end of that period I, Nebuchadnezzar, raised
> my eyes toward heaven, and my reason returned to
> me, and I blessed the Most High and praised and
> honored Him who lives forever. . . . Now I, Nebuchad-
> nezzar, praise, exalt, and honor the king of Heaven,
> for all His works are true and His ways just, and He is
> able to humble those who walk in pride." (vv. 34a, 37)

3. "It is interesting to find Daniel advising the king to seek to avert the coming disaster by
the practice of meritorious works. . . . It is unfortunate when the Christian doctrine of justifi-
cation by faith is presented in such a way that the challenge of the moral law is obscured.
The problem is to find the right place for morality. . . . Good works are not to be despised.
What Christianity supplies is a new motive for performing them." Norman Porteous, *Daniel*
(London, England: SCM Press, 1965), pp. 71–72.

Like Nebuchadnezzar, some of you might be stuck out in the field. And God is hack, hack, hacking away at your branches . . . cutting you down to size, ripping the scepter from your clutches. But God will restore you with *His* authority if you will say with Nebuchadnezzar:

"All the inhabitants of the earth are accounted
as nothing,
But He does according to *His will* in the host of
heaven." (v. 35a, emphasis added)

It's not too late to recognize the pronouns—*His* dominion, *His* kingdom, *His* will (v. 34b, see James 4:10).

III. Hearing the Kingdom Proclaimed

Before ascending to heaven, Jesus gathered His disciples to give them His last words. After all they had been through during the past forty days—watching their Savior die, then seeing Him resurrected— no doubt they were weary. So Jesus called the team into a huddle and gave them a halftime pep talk. For the second half, Jesus was putting a new strategy into the playbook: the Holy Spirit. And the Spirit would give them the second wind they needed to go out and win the world for Christ. He reminded them who would have the authority, even when they were being persecuted and cursed and rebuked. He talked about the kingdom. But had they yet internalized the term *kingdom?* Looking at five literary cameos from the book of Acts will answer this question and help fill out our own definition of the term. We will take only a brief look at each portrait, for in the next lesson we will study the same snapshots more closely.

A. Acts 8:10–13. Simon was a magician who had been esteemed in Samaritan eyes as "the Great Power of God." But when Philip the apostle preached "the good news about the kingdom," Simon reached out to God and was saved.

> And even Simon himself believed; and after being baptized, he continued on with Philip; and as he observed signs and great miracles taking place, he was constantly amazed. (v. 13)

The observation is clear: *The message of the kingdom diminishes all other powers.* When confronted with God's power, even Simon— a man with magical power—fell on his face to worship God.

B. Acts 14:19–22. Paul, still black and blue from his stoning in Lystra, returned to the scene to bring his kingdom message.

> They stoned Paul and dragged him out of the city, supposing him to be dead. But while the disciples stood around him, he arose and entered the city. And

the next day he went away with Barnabas to Derbe.
And after they had preached the gospel to that city
and had made many disciples, they returned to Lystra
and to Iconium and to Antioch, strengthening the
souls of the disciples, encouraging them to continue
in the faith, and saying, "Through many tribulations
we must enter the kingdom of God."

From this cameo we can observe that *kingdom living includes many tribulations.* F. B. Meyer comments:

If in an unknown country, I am informed that I must
pass through a valley where the sun is hidden, or
over a stony bit of road, to reach my abiding place—
when I come to it, each moment of shadow or jolt
of the carriage tells me that I am on the right road.[4]

Checkup

Do you ever get rained on? Ever get stuck in life's pot-
holes? If not, maybe you're on the wrong road. There is
no easy street when you're following Christ, and the toll
along the way is suffering (Phil. 1:29, 3:10; 1 Pet. 2:21, 4:19).
As George Macdonald reminds us: "The Son of Man suffered
unto the death, not that men might not suffer, but that their
sufferings might be like His."[5]

C. Acts 19:8–9. In Corinth—the kingdom of culture, sophistica-
tion, and art—Paul spent three months "reasoning and persuading them about the kingdom of God." When the Corinthians found
out that kingdom living required them to give up their rights,
they became "hardened and disobedient, speaking evil of the
Way before the multitude" (v. 9). So Paul gathered up his little
pocket of disciples and went to Tyrannus, where they began a
church. Looking at this New Testament vignette yields another
observation: *Kingdom emphasis thins the ranks.* It separates the
superficial onlookers from the serious disciples.

D. Acts 20:22–27. In this scene, Paul is determined to leave his
friends at Miletus en route to Jerusalem, knowing that only bondage and affliction await him. In verse 24, he explains the reason
for his fortitude.

"But I do not consider my life of any account as dear
to myself. . . ."

---

4. F. B. Meyer, *Christ in Isaiah* (Grand Rapids, Mich.: Zondervan Publishing House, 1970), p. 9.

5. George Macdonald in C. S. Lewis's *The Problem of Pain* (New York, N.Y.: The Macmillan Co., 1970).

Only a man with kingdom perspective could say this and remain honest. Paul goes on to further unravel the meaning of *kingdom*.

"And now, behold, I know that all of you, among whom I went about preaching *the kingdom*, will see my face no more. Therefore I testify to you this day, that I am innocent of the blood of all men. For I did not shrink from declaring to you *the whole purpose of God.*" (vv. 25–27, emphasis added)

In this monologue, Paul links God's kingdom with God's purpose. The observation stands boldly: *The kingdom is central to the whole purpose of God.*

E. Acts 28:23. Here Paul is under house arrest in Rome, talking to a crowd of people who have come to see him. Notice what he chooses to tell them.

... and he was explaining to them by solemnly testifying about the kingdom of God, and trying to persuade them concerning Jesus, from both the Law of Moses and from the Prophets, from morning until evening.

Notice, too, that the same two messages stayed on his heart during his entire imprisonment.

And he stayed two full years in his own rented quarters, and was welcoming all who came to him, preaching the kingdom of God, and teaching concerning the Lord Jesus Christ. (vv. 30–31)

These passages cameo another observation: *The kingdom is inseparably linked to the Lord Jesus Christ.* All conversation about the kingdom, however unobtrusive, invariably winds its way to the lordship of Christ. And the signposts along the way tell us to give up all we have in order to accept all He has to give us.

All or Nothing

We squirm inside whenever we're asked to throw ourselves completely into any one thing. And sometimes, rightly so. In the case of the father who's asked to sacrifice everything for his company ... the athlete who's required to give up everything for the team ... the doctor who's called on to abandon everything for the practice—overcommitment often needs to be wrestled to the ground. But when it comes to the kingdom commitment of surrendering our lives to God, we're best off holding nothing back. We can never obey God too fully—never love Jesus too deeply—never relinquish too much. Never.

20

🐦 *Living Insights*

What's the big deal about the kingdom? The big deal is that the kingdom is God's place of authority and the realm of His dominion. There are numerous references to the kingdom in the Scriptures, as we have already seen. Let's check out a few more.

- One of a Bible student's best friends is a concordance. Within its pages are listings of words along with their references. Look up the word *kingdom* and focus on the New Testament references. Using the same pattern we developed in the lesson, write down the reference and state a *principle* that corresponds with the verse.

The Kingdom	
Verses	Principles

Continued on next page

Study Two

Discovering scriptural observations about the kingdom is an important exercise in understanding God's authority. But that exercise is just the first step in the process. The next step is to *apply* these things to your life.

• Refer to the chart you completed on the previous page. What applications can you make based on the principles you established? Use the chart below to write out your thoughts. But remember—it's vital that you go beyond writing to actually applying these kingdom truths to your life.

The Kingdom	
Principles	Applications

It Involves His Kingdom
(Part Two)
Luke 19:1–27; Acts 8:10–13, 14:21–22, 19:8–9

Each decade, like a feature film headed for the big screen, is incomplete without its actors, setting, props, costumes, and theme song. Together, these express the tone of the times.

The sixties. The actors—"hippies"—wore as little as possible, and what they did wear was tattered and tie-dyed. Passion burned like incense in the communal air. Microphoned by Bob Dylan, Simon and Garfunkel, and the Beatles, their psychedelic feelings of love and peace and freedom expressed themselves everywhere—in their music, their art, even on bathroom walls. Their theme song was "All You Need Is Love."[1] They were committed to reaching out to other human beings, getting involved in social causes, and rebelling hard against anything that threatened their utopian ideals. Their thinking was centrifugal—outward and other-oriented.

The eighties. The "yuppies"—young, upwardly mobile professionals— star in this decade. Staged in a complex of high-rise condos, this era reeks with a dress-for-success, look-out-for-number-one attitude. The props are sushi and Perrier, BMWs and tanning oils. Their theme song is synthesized jazz on compact discs, piped through hi-tech stereo systems. Committed to their own success, these power seekers climb the corporate ladder hand over hand, rung for rung, knocking away anything that threatens to hinder their ascent. Yuppie thinking is centripetal—like a draining hot tub whose water is sucked into the center.

The humanistic aura of our times inevitably seeps in to poison our thinking. We cannot live completely unaffected by it. So, too, living in God's spiritual kingdom cannot help but affect us, change us. In this lesson we will see how kingdom living is sure to dilute our baneful philosophies and purify the turbid tributary of our minds.

I. A Few Reminders
Before building on the foundation of the last lesson, we will retighten our grip on a few of the kingdom's nuts and bolts.

A. The meaning of the kingdom. In John 3:3, Jesus explains to Nicodemus that we must enter the kingdom by a new birth . . . that we will never experience it through the warmth of the womb.
> ". . . unless one is born again, he cannot see the kingdom of God."

---

1. "All You Need Is Love" by John Lennon and Paul McCartney (Northern Songs Limited, 1967). All rights for the U.S., Canada, and Mexico controlled and administered by Blackwood Music under license from ATV Music (Maclen). All rights reserved. International copyright secured. Used by permission.

Just what is this kingdom? It's God's authority over our lives. It's His supreme right to rule. It's letting Him call the shots, unbegrudgingly. We enter the kingdom by a new birth, and we thrive in it by a constant pursuit of righteousness.

"But seek first His kingdom and His righteousness; and all these things shall be added to you." (Matt. 6:33; see also Matt. 5:6, Luke 1:74–75)

How different from the "me-first" message of the yuppies—or even the "others-first" cry of the hippies. In God's kingdom, God is first.

B. Our struggle with the kingdom. Luke 19 tells two stories that evidence first-century yuppie-ism. One shows a man released from the clutches of his own will by the accepting words of Jesus (v. 5); the other shows a group of slaves who chose to resist the tug of the kingdom. The first story is a true one. It's about Zaccheus—a rip-off tax collector impassioned by riches, who from the branch of a sycamore tree decided to relinquish his selfish striving. Listen to his words of repentance:

"Behold, Lord, half of my possessions I will give to the poor, and if I have defrauded anyone of anything, I will give back four times as much." (v. 8)

Jesus' response reveals His mission:

"Today salvation has come to this house, ... for the Son of Man has come to seek and to save that which was lost." (vv. 9–10)

The Example of Jesus

Jesus did not come to dazzle us with His power, nor to manipulate people or make Himself a name. He didn't come to manufacture success. He came to seek and to save the lost. He came to give up His rights so that the Father's will would be done (Luke 22:42). Jesus' image shines before our eyes. Are you mirroring His example? Or are you reflecting—maybe in whispered defiance—your own self-will?

Therefore be imitators of God, as beloved children; and walk in love, just as Christ also loved you, and gave Himself up for us, an offering and a sacrifice to God as a fragrant aroma. (Eph. 5:1–2)

The second story is a parable. It was Jesus' way of giving Zaccheus his first instruction in righteousness.

"A certain nobleman went to a distant country to receive a kingdom for himself, and then return. And he called ten of his slaves, and gave them ten minas,[2] and said to them, 'Do business with this until I come back.' But his citizens hated him, and sent a delegation after him, saying, *We do not want this man to reign over us.*' " (Luke 19:12–14, emphasis added)

This is the response many give today when asked to live under the lordship of Christ. Notice the seriousness of the slaves' rebellion in the nobleman's eyes:

"But these enemies of mine, who did not want me to reign over them, bring them here and slay them in my presence." (v. 27)

Losers Take All

Like the slaves, Zaccheus wrestled with the kingdom. But when he came face-to-face with his kind opponent—the Lord Jesus—he surrendered on the mat. It was Jesus who won the match, but it was Zaccheus who took home the trophy.

Are you saved, but still struggling on the mat, sweating and grunting, trying to avert Jesus' authority with quick, cunning moves?

The King will never pin you. But as long as you refuse to forfeit the match against the kingdom, your trophy will be an inner thirst that even Gatorade can never quench.

II. Some Important Applications

Let's take a closer look at the snapshots we glanced at in the last lesson. This will help us round out what we observed about the kingdom with some personal applications—applications that may make us squirm a little.

A. Acts 8:10–24. The story of Simon the magician—the man known as the Great Power of God—shows us how to apply the kingdom to our lives. Notice the lesson he learned about the kingdom:

> But when they believed Philip preaching the good news about the kingdom of God and the name of Jesus Christ, they were being baptized, men and women alike. And even Simon himself believed; and

2. "When used in a monetary sense, the *māneh* of silver was worth about . . . $34; the gold *māneh* was equal to about . . . $510." H. Porter in *The International Standard Bible Encyclopedia,* ed. James Orr (Grand Rapids, Mich.: William B. Eerdmans Publishing Co., 1956), p. 1981.

after being baptized, he continued on with Philip; and as he observed signs and great miracles taking place, he was constantly amazed. . . . Then they began laying their hands on them, and they were receiving the Holy Spirit. (vv. 12–13, 17)

Simon was so arrested by their miraculous works that he, too, wanted a piece of the pie.

Now when Simon saw that the Spirit was bestowed through the laying on of the apostles' hands, he offered them money, saying, "Give this authority to me as well, so that everyone on whom I lay my hands may receive the Holy Spirit." (vv. 18–19)

But Peter's words of rebuke grabbed Simon by the nape of the neck:

"May your silver perish with you, because you thought you could obtain the gift of God with money! You have no part or portion in this matter, for your heart is not right before God. Therefore repent of this wickedness of yours, and pray the Lord that if possible, the intention of your heart may be forgiven you. For I see that you are in the gall of bitterness and in the bondage of iniquity." (vv. 20–23)

Like a scolded puppy, Simon whimpered a tail-between-the-legs response.

Simon answered and said, "Pray to the Lord for me yourselves, so that nothing of what you have said may come upon me." (v. 24)

The application can be drawn: *When facing the temptation to make a name, call on kingdom power.*

⌐ I Wonder

You know, Lord, how I serve You
With great emotional fervor
In the limelight.
You know how eagerly I speak for You
At a women's club.
You know how I effervesce when I promote
A fellowship group.
You know my genuine enthusiasm
At a Bible study.

But how would I react, I wonder
If You pointed to a basin of water
And asked me to wash the calloused feet
Of a bent and wrinkled old woman

Day after day
Month after month
In a room where nobody saw
And nobody knew.[3]

B. Acts 14:21–22. Moving from Samaria to Lystra, we find another application that is hard to swallow. After his stoning in Lystra, Paul brushed himself off and traveled to Derbe to proclaim the gospel message. Notice the next spot on Paul's travel itinerary:

> And after they had preached the gospel to that city
> and had made many disciples, they returned to Lystra.
> (v. 21a)

He returned to the very place where he had been stoned! And observe what he did there:

> They returned to Lystra . . . strengthening the souls
> of the disciples, encouraging them to continue in the
> faith, and saying, "Through many tribulations we
> must enter the kingdom of God." (vv. 21b–22)

The message on Paul's heart was *suffering*—a message loathed by every person who wants an easy road and instant gratification. But to be part of the kingdom is to suffer. "And indeed, all who desire to live godly in Christ Jesus will be persecuted" (2 Tim. 3:12; see also Phil. 1:29, 1 Pet. 3:14). The application? *When going through times of testing, count on kingdom endurance.*

A Badge to Bear

In *The Cost of Commitment,* John White exposes what kingdom suffering is—and what it is not.

> Christian suffering has to do with the cross
> I take up and heave on my back. It is suffering
> because of a deliberate choice. The kind of cross
> to which Christ refers is not a "cross" of rheu-
> matism or of the petty annoyances that older
> evangelicals used to label their "cross in life."
> It is the badge of a true follower of Jesus. It may
> take any form—sickness, hunger, loneliness,
> persecution, death. It has been the glory of the
> church for two thousand years. . . . The words
> of the Lord of the church come ringing across

---

3. Ruth Harms Calkin, "I Wonder," from *Tell Me Again, Lord, I Forget* (Wheaton, Ill.: Tyndale House Publishers, 1986), p. 14. Used by permission.

27

the centuries. "Be faithful unto death, and I will give you a crown of life" (Rev. 2:10).[4]

C. Acts 19:8–9. Now in Ephesus, Paul brought his kingdom message into the synagogue.

> And he entered the synagogue and continued speaking out boldly for three months, reasoning and persuading them about the kingdom of God. (v. 8)

Speaking, reasoning, persuading. Why the strong verbs to describe Paul's ministry to the Ephesians?[5] Because they were not easily touched by talk about the kingdom. Their hearts were hardened—calloused and cold.

> But when some were becoming hardened[6] and disobedient, speaking evil of the Way before the multitude, he withdrew from them and took away the disciples, reasoning daily in the school in Tyrannus. (v. 9)

Because of the hard-heartedness of the Ephesians, Paul and the disciples left to start a church in Tyrannus. There's an important application to be made from this account: *When wondering why some walk away, realize that the kingdom separates.*

D. Acts 20:17–27. Here we see Paul in the little town of Miletus, bidding tearful good-byes to the elders of the church at Ephesus. He said to them,

> "And now, behold, I know that all of you, among whom I went about preaching the kingdom, will see my face no more. Therefore I testify to you this day, that I am innocent of the blood of all men. For I did not shrink from declaring to you the whole purpose of God." (vv. 25–27)

In this me-first generation, it's easy to shrink from the kingdom message, for it requires long-term commitment and self-sacrifice.

> For the time will come when they will not endure sound doctrine; but wanting to have their ears tickled, they will accumulate for themselves teachers in accordance to their own desires. (2 Tim. 4:3)

But kingdom living—the message that cuts so deeply into the lives of those who hear it—lies at the core of God's purpose.

---

4. John White, *The Cost of Commitment* (Downers Grove, Ill.: InterVarsity Press, 1976), pp. 12–13.

5. *Speaking* means "to declare as if making a proclamation." *Reasoning* means "dialoguing," which includes the ideas of "pondering" and "debating." And *persuading* means "to prevail upon so as to bring about a change."

6. *Hardened* means "dry" and conveys the idea of being austere and stern and severe.

The application is clear: *When coming to terms with the whole purpose of God, remember kingdom commitment.*

E. Acts 28:23-24, 30-31. Here we find Paul sharing his faith with people who were anxious to hear about it.

> ...and he was explaining to them by solemnly testifying about the kingdom of God, and trying to persuade them concerning Jesus. (v. 23a)

Verses 30-31 show the content of Paul's message:

> And he stayed two full years in his own rented quarters, ...preaching the kingdom of God, and teaching concerning the Lord Jesus Christ with all openness, unhindered.

The kingdom and the Lord Jesus Christ are two inseparable links in the chain of faith. The application: *When sharing your faith, include kingdom authority.*

A Concluding Application

Like the hippies of the sixties and the yuppies of the eighties, cast members of God's kingdom all read the same script. The set combines heavenly principles with earthly realities. The props are the fruits of righteousness and peace and joy (Rom. 14:17). The cast may be costumed in frayed cutoffs or tweed blazers, but all of them are clothed in the righteousness of Jesus. The kingdom requires neither the idealistic rebellion of the sixties nor the casual self-absorption of the eighties. It asks for a surrendered will, an acknowledgment of God's authority over every area of our lives. Is the theme song of your life "Have Thine Own Way, Lord"?[7] Is His purpose your purpose—His will, your will? If not, Jesus is waiting for you to descend your heart's throne and let Him be king ... and make the glories of His kingdom a reality in your life.

> The kingdom of heaven is like a treasure hidden in the field, which a man found and hid; and from joy over it he goes and sells all that he has, and buys that field. (Matt. 13:44)[8]

Continued on next page

---

7. "Have Thine Own Way, Lord!" Words by Adelaide A. Pollard.

8. For a poignant description of the kingdom, see John White's *The Cost of Commitment*, pp. 46–50.

Living Insights

If we seriously desire to follow Christ, we must allow kingdom teachings to penetrate our personal lives. Use the space provided to write how you will *personalize* each of the five applications from this lesson. Begin by asking yourself, What difference can this principle make in my life?

- When facing the temptation to make a name, call on kingdom power.

_____

_____

_____

_____

- When going through times of testing, count on kingdom endurance.

_____

_____

_____

_____

- When wondering why some walk away, realize that the kingdom separates.

_____

_____

_____

_____

- When coming to terms with the whole purpose of God, remember kingdom commitment.

_____

_____

_____

_____

- When sharing your faith, include kingdom authority.

_____

_____

_____

_____

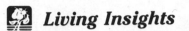 *Living Insights*

What does it take to experience God's kingdom? In brief, it takes giving the King full authority over every part of your life. Easy to say—harder to live out.

- There's a tremendously important issue at stake here. It's well worth our time to think through an answer. *How can kingdom living help me live above the level of mediocrity?* Write your thoughts in the space provided. Be as specific as you can.

Kingdom Living—Life Above Mediocrity

_____

_____

_____

_____

_____

_____

_____

_____

_____

_____

_____

It Costs Your Commitment
Luke 14:25–35

Great leaders are people who clearly state the cost of the commitment their followers must make—no matter how demanding or dangerous that commitment might be.

King Arthur was such a leader. His knights came to him with zeal and enthusiasm, but he bound them to himself with vows that required the highest level of devotion.

"Arthur sat
Crown'd on the daïs, and his warriors cried,
'Be thou the king, and we will work thy will
Who love thee.' Then the King in low deep tones,
And simple words of great authority,
Bound them by so strait vows to his own self,
That when they rose, knighted from kneeling, some
Were pale as at the passing of a ghost,
Some flush'd, and others dazed, as one who wakes
Half-blinded at the coming of a light."[1]

No leader required such "strait vows" of loyalty as Jesus. If the people were to follow Him, they would have to count the cost . . . for the cost would be exacting.

I. The Setting
Multitudes flocked wherever Jesus went (Luke 14:25). Some were drawn to His simple stories and clear teaching about spiritual things; others came in hopes of being healed. Still others came out of curiosity, hoping to see some miracle . . . like crowds hovering around the scene of an accident, craning their necks to see the out-of-the-ordinary. Patriots also came—those who, under the restive dominion of Rome, were eager to find a young revolutionary whom they might recruit as a spokesman for their cause.

II. The Terms of Consecration
Looking over the sea of faces that followed Him, Jesus—like King Arthur—explicitly stated the terms of consecration which He required of His disciples (vv. 26–27, 33).

A. Personal relationships. The first and most stringent of the terms is found in verse 26.

"If anyone comes to Me, and does not hate his own father and mother and wife and children and brothers

---

1. Allan Knee, ed., *Idylls of the King* AND *Camelot* (New York, N.Y.: Dell Publishing Co., 1967), p. 25.

and sisters, yes, and even his own life, he cannot be
My disciple."

No one could ever accuse Christ of beating around the bush or
hedging on tough issues. No election-year politics here. Just the
truth, unsheathed and unblunted. But *hate?* Such a staggering
word. Yet that was His intention—to stagger the crowds, to thin
the uncommitted from the ranks. In dramatic fashion, Jesus
stated the primary condition for discipleship. In the realm of
relationships, *He must come first.*

> He who wishes to follow Him must choose Him so
> unconditionally as Lord and Guide that he makes all
> other loyalties and ties absolutely subordinate to his
> loyalty and devotion to Him. The Saviour, of course,
> does not mean that he who desires to follow Him
> must hate his parents and other loved ones as such,
> but certainly that if loyalty to Him clashes with loy-
> alty to them he is to treat his loved ones in this con-
> nection *as though* they are persons whom he hates.[2]

Jesus asks for nothing less than our hearts—which cannot be
given in halves (see Matt. 6:24, 10:37). All relationships, no matter
how intimate, must be secondary to our relationship with Christ.

> To hate one's family means to be so committed to
> Christ that however much it costs me to be away from
> that circle, I must cut myself ruthlessly from its com-
> fort and follow Him barefoot on rocky pathways.[3]

B. Personal desires. Expanding on the words "even his own
life," Jesus told His followers that to be His disciples they must
be willing to sacrifice even the most personal of desires.

> "Whoever does not carry his own cross and come after
> Me cannot be My disciple." (Luke 14:27)

As these Roman ruled Palestinians heard His words, they must
have pictured the all-too-familiar scene of criminals trudging to
their execution, carrying on their shoulders the very crosses on
which they were to suffer. Jesus confronted His listeners with
the reality that following Him could cost them their lives—
literally. And He offered no padding to cushion their shoulders
from the splinters of that cross and no anesthesia for the nails.
In Romans 12:1, Paul employs a similar metaphor to paint with
bold strokes the stark black-and-white realities of discipleship.

2. Norval Geldenhuys, *Commentary on the Gospel of Luke* (Grand Rapids, Mich.: William B.
Eerdmans Publishing Co., 1972), p. 398. See also Deuteronomy 13:6–10 for an example of how
a clash in loyalties between family and God was to be handled under the old covenant.

3. John White, *The Cost of Commitment* (Downers Grove, Ill.: InterVarsity Press, 1976), p. 62.

> I urge you therefore, brethren, by the mercies of God, to present your bodies a living and holy sacrifice, acceptable to God, which is your spiritual service of worship.

Carrying our cross means charting a path that, every step of the way, leads to death. Death to self. Our will, our goals, our desires are all to be nailed to a cross. Paul tells us that Christ died so that "they who live should no longer live for themselves" (2 Cor. 5:15) but should live in such a way as "to be pleasing to Him" (v. 9). And, modeled after Christ, this new ambition will change our relationships with those around us.

> Now we who are strong ought to bear the weaknesses of those without strength and not just please ourselves. Let each of us please his neighbor for his good, to his edification. For even Christ did not please Himself. (Rom. 15:1–3a)

The Way of the Cross

Have you taken that painful walk to Calvary with your goals and desires and dreams? Have you honestly and objectively taken them before the Lord for His approval? Do they feed your ego more than they honor Him? Are you willing to change them if God shows you that you should?

It is an agonizing task to play the executioner on your life's ambitions—to pound the nails and lift the cross. But just remember: after crucifixion comes resurrection. And out of a cold tomb, God will raise goals and desires warm with new life and power.

> Delight yourself in the Lord;
> And He will give you the desires of your heart.
> (Ps. 37:4)

C. Personal possessions. The third stipulation Jesus insists upon for His followers is a loose grip on all earthly possessions.

> "So therefore, no one of you can be My disciple who does not give up all his own possessions." (Luke 14:33)

If the hand on your possessions is clenched tight, Jesus will not be able to take that hand and lead you very far. At some point, clinging to possessions will pull you away from Christ. Whether a nice house, a new car, or an Ivy League education . . . if held too tightly, possessions will hold you back from fully following Christ. Is there something in your life that you can't seem to let go of? Do you want it so badly that you don't really possess it anymore, but it possesses you? If the Lord ever chooses to take it, the loss will be a lot less painful if you relax your grip.

A Quote to Remember

"The chaos of our lesser loyalties cries aloud for some regal loyalty to rule them. Oh, for some transcendent passion—as pure as purity, as loving as love—to gather all other worthy passions beneath the healing of its wings!"[4]

III. The Reasons for Consecration

Christ's disciples have Him as their foremost love and have themselves and their possessions in proper perspective behind Him. But why did Christ state the terms of consecration with such exactness? The reason is found in verses 28–32.

A. The parable of the improvident builder. In verses 28–30, Jesus brought His point home with an illustration each listener could relate to.

> "For which one of you, when he wants to build a tower, does not first sit down and calculate the cost, to see if he has enough to complete it? Otherwise, when he has laid a foundation, and is not able to finish, all who observe it begin to ridicule him, saying, 'This man began to build and was not able to finish.'"

The Herods had a passion for erecting elaborate works of architecture. Doubtless, many whose resources were more limited tried to imitate them and ended up with their bank accounts depleted and their buildings unfinished. Pilate, for instance, had begun building an aqueduct which, from lack of funds, was left incomplete. Here Jesus uses the example of a tower, which begins as a challenge to the sky and ends up the unsightly stubble of an improvident venture, becoming a target for ridicule. How about you? If the blueprint is the Sermon on the Mount and the cost is everything you hold dear in life, are you willing to build a life that will stand as a towering testimony for Jesus?

B. The parable of the unprepared king. In a similar illustration found in verses 31–32, Jesus emphasizes His point.

> "Or what king, when he sets out to meet another king in battle, will not first sit down and take counsel whether he is strong enough with ten thousand men to encounter the one coming against him with twenty

---

4. George A. Butterick, *The Parables of Jesus* (New York, N.Y.: Harper and Brothers Publishers, 1928), p. 81.

thousand? Or else, while the other is still far away, he sends a delegation and asks terms of peace."

The message of the parable is clear: Do not undertake what you have neither the strength nor the will nor the resources to accomplish. The war of the Christian is fought on many fronts—with the world, the flesh, and the Devil. The battle is ruthless. The bullets are real. And the commitment of the soldier determines whether victory or surrender will be the final outcome.

A Word to the Troops

Sir Winston Churchill addressed the House of Commons on October 8, 1940, regarding the war with Hitler. In sobering words similar to Christ's, he prepared his followers for the battle.

> Death and sorrow will be the companions of our journey; hardship our garment; constancy and valor our only shield.[5]

In wartime, soldiers must forego many of the privileges, pleasures, and possessions of the common people. Not because these things are wrong, but because the more pressing priorities of the war demand their sacrifice.

IV. The Summary

In verses 34–35, Jesus crystallizes His teaching with a metaphor.

"Therefore, salt is good; but if even salt has become tasteless, with what will it be seasoned? It is useless either for the soil or for the manure pile; it is thrown out. He who has ears to hear, let him hear."

Salt is valuable only when it possesses that special, unique quality of saltiness. Similarly, followers of Jesus are only of practical value when they possess that particular characteristic of Christlikeness.[6]

Something to Think About

Life is like a coin. You can spend it any way you like, but you can only spend it once. How are you spending yours?

---

5. *Bartlett's Familiar Quotations,* 14th ed., rev. and enl., ed. Emily Morison Beck (Boston, Mass.: Little, Brown and Co., 1968), p. 921.

6. The character qualities of Christlikeness are pictured in the mosaic commonly referred to as the Beatitudes, found in Matthew 5:1–11. Compare this with verse 13.

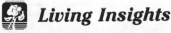

Living Insights

As our study progresses, we find ourselves digging deeper into the subject of mediocrity. In this lesson we learned about the cost of commitment. Are you willing to pay the price?

● We've been concentrating on Luke 14:25–35. This passage is rich with detail concerning the cost of commitment. Let's analyze the passage by asking some pointed questions.

1. Who is Jesus talking to? _____

_____

_____

2. What is He asking them to do? _____

_____

_____

3. Why is He asking them to do this? _____

_____

_____

4. What does this mean for me? _____

_____

_____

Living Insights

In this lesson we looked at three terms of consecration. They involve yielding to God our relationships, desires, and possessions. Does your life meet the criteria?

● How does your relationship with God compare to your relationships with these people?

Father _____

_____

Continued on next page

37

Mother _____

_____

Mate _____

_____

Brothers _____

_____

Sisters _____

_____

Children _____

_____

- How do your desires compare to God's desires for you? Take a few minutes to think about each of the following questions.
  —Have I honestly and objectively taken my life's goals before the Lord for His approval?
  —Do my goals feed my ego more than they honor the Lord?
  —Am I willing to change my goals if God shows me that I should?
- Make a brief list of your possessions and put a check (√) by the ones you've consecrated to God. What about the others? What is keeping you from giving them to God? Take some time to ask God to help you trust Him with those things.

My Possessions

_____   _____

_____   _____

_____   _____

_____   _____

_____   _____

_____   _____

_____   _____

_____   _____

It Calls for Extravagant Love
Mark 14:1–9

Many years ago, a tourist group made its way through the house where the great composer Ludwig van Beethoven spent his last years. Reaching his conservatory, the guide paused and whispered reverently, "And here is the master's instrument."

One of the tourists, a woman, pushed her way to the piano. She sat down at the bench and began to play one of Beethoven's sonatas. "I suppose a lot of people love to play this piano," she remarked.

The guide placed his hand on hers, stilling her music. "Well, when Ignacy Paderewski was here last summer, he was asked to play by several people. But he responded, 'Oh, no! I am not worthy to play the same keyboard as the great Beethoven.'"

Similarly, some scenes in Scripture seem too sacred to touch. Some are majestic psalms of praise; others, like the one we'll view today, are sublime moments of simple devotion.

So, with a reverent hush, let's tiptoe back in time. We'll visit the house where Jesus spent one of His last days, and we'll eavesdrop on a moment of pure, extravagant love.

I. Setting the Scene
The backdrop to this expression of extravagant love juxtaposes tradition with treachery, religious observance with ruthless opposition.
   A. The time. Our travel takes us to Jerusalem during the Passover celebration just before Christ's crucifixion.

> Now the Passover and Unleavened Bread was two days off; and the chief priests and the scribes were seeking how to seize Him by stealth, and kill Him; for they were saying, "Not during the festival, lest there be a riot of the people." (Mark 14:1–2)[1]

What the Fourth of July is to America, Passover was to ancient Israel, only more so. It was a time of celebrating heartily, of singing great Jewish songs, of reenacting the drama of Israel's deliverance from Egypt. Jews from all over made the pilgrimage to Jerusalem each year to celebrate this pinnacle of religious holidays.
   B. The atmosphere. At this particular Passover, however, the mood of some is not so festive. Instead of celebrating, a few influential religious leaders are planning an execution. The atmosphere is tense, and the situation delicate, for, as John notes, "many

---

1. The word *stealth* in verse 1 means "a trick or surprise attack."

of the Jews were . . . believing in Jesus" (John 12:11). If the plan isn't smoothly and surreptitiously carried out, it could backfire in their faces.

C. **The place.** Suddenly we find ourselves transported a few miles from that scene in Jerusalem to a modest home in Bethany.

> And while He was in Bethany at the home of Simon the leper, and reclining at the table . . . (Mark 14:3a)

The home of Simon, the leper whom Jesus had cleansed, serves as one of the final respites for the Savior before He will at last rest His head on the splintered roughness of the cross.

D. **The people.** John fills in a few of the story's more personal details by listing Simon's dinner guests for us. He has invited not only Lazarus, whom Jesus recently raised from the dead, but also Lazarus's sisters, Martha and Mary, along with Judas Iscariot and probably several, if not all, of the other disciples (John 12:1–11).

II. Devotion and Reaction

Into this serene setting a woman silently enters, and she shows the Savior an extravagant display of love.

A. **The woman.**

> There came a woman with an alabaster vial of very costly perfume of pure nard;[2] and she broke the vial and poured it over His head. (Mark 14:3b)

The woman, John tells us, is Mary (John 12:3).[3] He also adds that she uses her hair to wipe His feet with the perfume.

B. **The observers.** The magnificence of this lavish display of love is marred by the murmur of some money-minded men.

> But some were indignantly remarking to one another, "Why has this perfume been wasted? For this perfume might have been sold for over three hundred denarii,[4] and the money given to the poor." And they were scolding her. (Mark 14:4–5)

On their utilitarian scale, extravagant devotion held little weight.

C. **The Lord.** Jesus intervened not only to stop the scolding but also to give special attention to Mary's devotion.

---

2. Genuine nard was made from dried leaves of a rare and unique Himalayan plant. The particular vase she used, if it was like others used in that day to hold expensive ointment, was itself a thing of beauty and held twelve ounces—a Roman pound (compare John 12:3).

3. Each of the three times we see Mary in the Bible, she is at the feet of Christ (Luke 10:39; John 11:32, 12:3).

4. A denarius was equivalent to a day's wage. Therefore, the perfume would have been worth almost a year's salary.

But Jesus said, "Let her alone; why do you bother her? She has done a good deed to Me. For the poor you always have with you, and whenever you wish, you can do them good; but you do not always have Me. She has done what she could; she has anointed My body beforehand for the burial." (vv. 6–8)

Death is the last subject anyone would want discussed at a dinner party. Talk about quenching a festive mood! But Mary had taken to heart Jesus' words about His imminent death (compare 10:32–34, 12:1–12). She didn't suppress the subject; she faced it—and it grieved her to the point of tears. Jesus saw her act of mourning as an early embalming. Doubtless, the fragrance drenched His garment and lingered in the fabric, reminding Him subtly—even in the midst of betrayal, desertion, denial, trials, beatings, mockings, and death—that there were those who loved Him. Purely. Deeply. And extravagantly!

A Time for Extravagance

How pure, how deep, how extravagant is your love for Christ?

If it were *your* bottle of perfume—a bottle that cost you a year's salary—would you have emptied it on the Savior? Or would you have sold it and given the money to the poor? Or kept it for yourself? Or would you have divided it— maybe ten percent for the Lord, a percentage for the poor, and the remainder for yourself?

To be sure, there is a time for prudence. But there is also a time for extravagance. There is a time to sell perfume for the poor. But there is also a time to shower it on the Lord.

III. A Lasting Memorial

According to John 12:3, the fragrance filled the room. And Jesus said that this aromatic moment, so pleasing to the nostrils of God, would linger through time as a subtly fragrant reminder of this woman's love.

"And truly I say to you, wherever the gospel is preached in the whole world, that also which this woman has done shall be spoken of in memory of her." (Mark 14:9)

Before you close the door on our lesson, take a deep breath and smell the aroma of extravagant love.

41

Broken Vases

The aroma of extravagant love.
So pure. So lovely.
Flowing from the veined alabaster vase
    of Mary's broken heart—
A heart broken against the hard reality
    of her Savior's imminent death.
Mingled with tears, the perfume became—
    by some mysterious chemistry of Heaven—
Not diluted, but more concentrated,
Potent enough behind the ears of each century
    for the scent to linger to this day.

Doubtless, the fragrance, absorbed by His garment,
    as it flowed from His head
Accompanied Christ through the humiliation of His trials,
                    the indignity of His mockings,
                    the pain of His beatings,
                    the inhumanity of His cross.
Through the heavy smell of sweat and blood,
A hint of that fragrance must have arisen
    from His garment—
Until, at shameful last, the garment was stripped
    and gambled away.
And maybe, just maybe, it was *that* scent
    amid the stench of humanity rabbled around the cross,
    that gave the Savior the strength to say:
"Father, forgive them, for they know not what they do."

And as Mary walked away from the cross,
The same scent probably still lingered in the now-limp hair
    she used to dry her Savior's feet—
A reminder of the love that spilled
    from His broken alabaster body.
So pure. So lovely.
So *truly* extravagant.

It was a vase He never regretted breaking.
Nor did she.

—Ken Gire

"But thanks be to God, who . . . manifests through us the sweet aroma of the knowledge of Him in every place. For we are a fragrance of Christ to God among those who are being saved and among those who are perishing" (2 Cor. 2:14–15).

🪶 Living Insights

One needs only a casual glance at Mark's account to realize the tone is one of thoughtful tenderness. It's a story of love's sweet expression. And it is beautiful.

- The story of Mary and her precious perfume appears not only in Mark 14 but also in Matthew 26:6–13 and John 12:1–8. Study the three versions of this event and fill in the chart that follows.

Extravagant Love	
Mark 14:1–9, Matthew 26:6–13, John 12:1–8	
Similarities	Differences

Continued on next page

⚘ *Living Insights*

Extravagance . . . so many thoughts and feelings are conjured up by that word. For many believers, their honest response is one of discomfort.

- Use the space below to write out your own philosophy of extravagance. What place does extravagance have in a Christian's life? How does your background influence your view?

How I View Extravagance

_____

_____

_____

_____

_____

_____

_____

_____

_____

_____

Vision: Seeing Beyond the Majority

Numbers 13:25–33, 14:6–9; Matthew 6:31–34

In his Harvard commencement address of June 8, 1978, Aleksandr Solzhenitsyn spoke against the majority like a prophet crying in the wilderness:

> A decline in courage may be the most striking feature that an outside observer notices in the West today. . . .
>
> Must one point out that from ancient times a decline in courage has been considered the first symptom of the end? . . .
>
> If the world has not approached its end, it has reached a major watershed in history, equal in importance to the turn from the Middle Ages to the Renaissance. It will demand from us a spiritual effort; we shall have to rise to a new height of vision.[1]

If we are ever to rise above mediocrity, we must have the vision to see beyond what the majority sees. Yet vision takes courage—courage to leave the majority behind at the foothills and scale the peaks of faith.

I. Living by Faith

Faith: the evidence of things not seen (see Heb. 11:1). Paul reminds us in 2 Corinthians 5:7 that, as Christians, "we walk by faith, not by sight." Since the kingdom of God is unseen, faith must be our eyes if we are ever to see beyond the material kingdom of this world. Anxiety about our material circumstances emotionally ties us to this world—and sometimes ties us in such knots that we are bound to a life of mediocrity. In the Sermon on the Mount, Jesus cuts these bonds loose so we can soar above the majority, above mediocrity.

> "Do not be anxious then, saying, 'What shall we eat?' or 'What shall we drink?' or 'With what shall we clothe ourselves?' For all these things the Gentiles eagerly seek; for your heavenly Father knows that you need all these things. But seek first His kingdom and His righteousness; and all these things shall be added to you. Therefore do not be anxious for tomorrow; for tomorrow will care for itself. Each day has enough trouble of its own." (Matt. 6:31–34)

II. Living by Courage

Courage: that muscle of character which flexes to give individuals, families, and nations their strength. To live above the level of mediocrity, we must live courageously. And none have lived more courageously than two men who stood up against the majority, against

1. Aleksandr I. Solzhenitsyn, *East and West* (New York, N.Y.: Harper and Row, 1980), pp. 44–45, 71.

the consensus of the nation of Israel. Two men who lived by faith rather than by sight. Men of vision. Their names: Joshua and Caleb.

A. The historical context of Numbers 13–14. Set free from their bondage to Pharaoh, the Israelites departed in a mass exodus from Egypt with all their belongings and family members. Under Moses' leadership, they arrived at the edge of Canaan. According to the last verse of Numbers 12, the Israelites "camped in the wilderness of Paran," right on the border of the Promised Land. In the Exodus, God bared His arm of salvation in a visual display of strength that should have convinced even the most spiritually nearsighted of His power: the plagues in Egypt ... the emancipation by Pharaoh ... the parting of the Red Sea ... the destruction of the Egyptian army.

B. The spy mission. Now, on the border of Canaan, the Israelites could actually see the land God had promised them. Their faith was literally materializing before their very eyes. Undoubtedly, their hearts raced and their spirits soared as they awaited Moses' orders. Then God instructed Moses:

> "Send out for yourself men so that they may spy out the land of Canaan, which I am going to give to the sons of Israel; you shall send a man from each of their fathers' tribes, every one a leader among them." So Moses sent them from the wilderness of Paran at the command of the Lord, all of them men who were heads of the sons of Israel.... When Moses sent them to spy out the land of Canaan, he said to them, "Go up there into the Negev; then go up into the hill country. And see what the land is like, and whether the people who live in it are strong or weak, whether they are few or many. And how is the land in which they live, is it good or bad? And how are the cities in which they live, are they like open camps or with fortifications? And how is the land, is it fat or lean? Are there trees in it or not? Make an effort then to get some of the fruit of the land." Now the time was the time of the first ripe grapes. (13:2–3, 17–20)

C. The majority report. The spies were on a reconnaissance mission. And when they returned, they had all the statistics they needed.

> They brought back word ... to all the congregation and showed them the fruit of the land. Thus they told him, and said, "We went in to the land where you sent us; and it certainly does flow with milk and honey, and this is its fruit." (vv. 26b–27)

But as sure as milk is smooth and honey is sweet, you can bet there's a bull behind the barn and bees within the hive.

> "Nevertheless, the people who live in the land are strong, and the cities are fortified and very large; and moreover, we saw the descendants of Anak there. Amalek is living in the land of the Negev and the Hittites and the Jebusites and the Amorites are living in the hill country, and the Canaanites are living by the sea and by the side of the Jordan." (vv. 28–29)

In the face of these frightening facts, one man of faith had the courage to speak out against the majority.

> Then Caleb quieted the people before Moses, and said, "We should by all means go up and take possession of it, for we shall surely overcome it." (v. 30)

But the majority—who lived by sight—pulled out their measuring sticks, which fated them to mediocrity.

> But the men who had gone up with him said, "We are not able to go up against the people, for they are too strong for us." So they gave out to the sons of Israel a bad report of the land which they had spied out, saying, "The land through which we have gone, in spying it out, is a land that devours its inhabitants; and all the people whom we saw in it are men of great size. There also we saw the Nephilim (the sons of Anak are part of the Nephilim); and we became like grasshoppers in our own sight, and so we were in their sight." (vv. 31–33)

The Challenge of Canaan

What is your Canaan? What is your challenge? Which giants make you feel like a grasshopper?

When we live by statistics, by comparing the odds, by numbering and measuring and weighing, the results are predictable: we become intimidated, crushed like grasshoppers by the giant heels of the challenges God has set before us.

And God gives us challenges, not to crush us, but to make us courageous.

D. The reaction to the majority report. The Grasshoppers against the Giants. Who do you think will win? Prediction: the Grasshoppers are gonna get squished—and get squished good! If you're making your choice by sizing up the competition, shoe sizes will always win out. Consequently, the people's reaction to the report was predictably bleak.

> Then all the congregation lifted up their voices and cried, and the people wept that night. And all the sons of Israel grumbled against Moses and Aaron; and the whole congregation said to them, "Would that we had died in the land of Egypt! Or would that we had died in this wilderness! And why is the Lord bringing us into this land, to fall by the sword? Our wives and our little ones will become plunder; would it not be better for us to return to Egypt?" So they said to one another, "Let us appoint a leader and return to Egypt." (14:1–4)

Majority rules, right? After all, that's very democratic, very "of the people, by the people, for the people." But history has proven that the majority is seldom right.

E. The minority report. The majority raised a white flag. Their proposal: "When things look bleak, retreat." But a minority of two raised a different flag—a battle flag. Their proposal: "When things look bleak, stop looking at *things* and start looking at *God!*"

> And Joshua the son of Nun and Caleb the son of Jephunneh, of those who had spied out the land, tore their clothes; and they spoke to all the congregation of the sons of Israel, saying, "The land which we passed through to spy out is an exceedingly good land. If the Lord is pleased with us, then He will bring us into this land, and give it to us—a land which flows with milk and honey. Only do not rebel against the Lord; and do not fear the people of the land, for they shall be our prey. Their protection has been removed from them, and the Lord is with us; do not fear them." (vv. 6–9)

Verses for the Battlefield

> The Lord is my light and my salvation;
> Whom shall I fear?
> The Lord is the defense of my life;
> Whom shall I dread?
> When evildoers came upon me to devour my flesh,
> My adversaries and my enemies, they stumbled and fell.
> Though a host encamp against me,

> My heart will not fear;
> Though war arise against me,
> In spite of this I shall be confident. (Ps. 27:1–3)

III. Living by Vision

Vision: the ability to see God's presence, power, and plan in spite of the obstacles. The alphabet of vision consists of attitude, belief, capacity, determination, and enthusiasm.

A. Attitude. When you have vision, your attitude is positive rather than negative, optimistic rather than pessimistic.

B. Belief. "Faith is the assurance of things hoped for, the conviction of things not seen" (Heb. 11:1). When you have vision, you have assurance and confidence—not only in God, but in others and in yourself.

C. Capacity. When you have vision, you demonstrate a willing capacity to be stretched. And Christians, like rubber bands, are never really useful until they are stretched.

D. Determination. When you have vision, you develop the determination to dig into the trenches and face hand-to-hand combat.

E. Enthusiasm. When you have vision, you have the enthusiastic perspective that God is in your corner—fighting for you, not against you.

An Example of Vision

"An American, visiting in France came upon a scene where a large church was being erected. He approached three stone masons, one after the other. Of each he asked this question: 'What are you doing?' The first replied: 'I'm cutting stone.' The second said: 'I'm cutting stone for seven francs a day.' The third responded: 'I'm helping to build a great cathedral.' "[2]

Can you see cathedrals in the challenges God has set before you—or just a lot of rough stones? Faith sees the cathedrals; sight sees the stones.

Continued on next page

2. Jacob M. Brande, *Speaker's Encyclopedia of Stories, Quotations, and Anecdotes* (Englewood Cliffs, N.J.: Prentice-Hall, 1955), p. 400.

 *Living Insights*

If you aspire to rise above the majority and their contagious mediocrity, you must possess the essential quality of *vision*. The story of Joshua and Caleb inspires us with God's view of vision. Let's probe further into this account.

● Paraphrasing is the art of putting something into your own words, which adds emotion and feeling to the text. Let's paraphrase the events recorded in Numbers 13 and 14. To maintain the story line, however, you may want to skip verses 4 through 16 of chapter 13.

My Paraphrase of Numbers 13 and 14

_____

_____

_____

_____

_____

_____

_____

_____

_____

_____

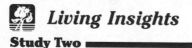 *Living Insights*

Would you like to live above mediocrity for the rest of your life? The key is gaining spiritual vision. It was spelled out for us in a simple formula of A-B-C-D-E. Let's review that part of the lesson and study each word. Then rate yourself honestly (5 being best, 1 being worst). Use the space provided to develop a plan for improvement in your weaker areas.

Attitude   1 2 3 4 5

_____

_____

_____

Belief   1 2 3 4 5

_____

_____

_____

Capacity   1 2 3 4 5

_____

_____

_____

Determination   1 2 3 4 5

_____

_____

_____

Enthusiasm   1 2 3 4 5

_____

_____

_____

Determination: Deciding to Hang Tough

Joshua 14:7–12, 23:6–7, 24:14–15

Potential. We all have it in some measure. Pools of it bubble beneath the surface of our lives, like untapped reservoirs of oil.

But to tap into that potential and bring it to the surface, we need to have the determination to drill. That takes not only faith enough to launch a risky venture but also persistence enough to keep drilling away, day after day, night after night—sometimes on a desolate rig.

Living above the level of mediocrity takes the determination to decide to hang tough—whether your drilling rig is on Alaska's North Slope, or on the frontier of your children's adolescent years, or in the blinding sandstorms of a marital Sahara. Excellence in life comes not so much from the gift of potential but from the guts of persistence.

> Press on: nothing in the world can take the place of persistence. Talent will not; nothing is more common than unsuccessful men with talent. Genius will not; unrewarded genius is almost a proverb. Education will not; the world is full of educated derelicts. Persistence and determination alone are overwhelmingly powerful.[1]

I. Definitions of Key Terms

Before we can drill any deeper into our topic, it is necessary to define some of the pivotal terms our study revolves around.

A. Vision. This is the ability to see beyond the majority. Vision is perception—reading the presence and power of God into our own circumstances. When we view life with vision, we perceive events and circumstances from God's perspective. The prophet Isaiah speaks of this divine perspective in Isaiah 55, verses 8–9:

> "For My thoughts are not your thoughts,
> Neither are your ways My ways," declares the Lord.
> "For as the heavens are higher than the earth,
> So are My ways higher than your ways,
> And My thoughts than your thoughts."

Seen through heavenly lenses, the things God views as important come into sharp relief. For example, take a look at a story in 1 Samuel 16. King Saul has failed as a leader, so God sends Samuel to find a new king. Coming to the home of Jesse, Samuel first examines Eliab, the oldest son, for the position. Eliab's

---

1. Calvin Coolidge, as quoted by Ted. W. Engstrom in *Motivation to Last a Lifetime* (Grand Rapids, Mich: Zondervan Publishing House, 1984), p. 76.

physical features are so impressive that Samuel feels sure he's found the Lord's anointed. But God corrects Samuel's blurred vision.

> "Do not look at his appearance or at the height of his stature, because I have rejected him; for God sees not as man sees, for man looks at the outward appearance, but the Lord looks at the heart." (v. 7)

Human vision focuses on externals and is easily impressed by appearances. Divine vision, on the other hand, looks beyond appearances into the hidden recesses of the heart.

B. Determination. This is faith for the long haul, disciplining ourselves to remain consistent regardless of the obstacles. A textbook example of determination can be found in the life of Daniel. Uprooted from his native land, Daniel was transplanted to the Hanging Gardens of Babylon where he served in King Nebuchadnezzar's court. Entrenched in foreign soil, Daniel had an iron-will determination to keep himself unsullied from the pagan influences there: "Daniel *made up his mind* that he would not defile himself" (Dan. 1:8a, emphasis added).

C. Dream. This is a God-given idea, plan, agenda, or goal that leads to God-honoring results. Dreams are specific and personal, not generally applied to the public. They are the hallmark of innovative leadership.

Take Time to Dream

Most of us don't dream enough. We just don't take the time. What if someone were to ask you, "What are your dreams for this year? What are your hopes . . . your agenda items? What are you trusting God for?" Could you give a specific answer?

Before responding, remember to look beyond your personal goals and objectives and think about your *God-given* dreams.

II. Illustrations of Two Who Dreamed

Turn now to Numbers 14. As you may recall from our last study, we saw two men who had vision, determination, and dreams—and ten who didn't. Ten men saw the problem; two saw the solution. Ten were impressed with the size of the enemy; two were impressed with the size of their God. Ten believed victory couldn't be achieved; two believed victory would come through the promise and power of God.

A. Before the fight. Joshua and Caleb's speech to the congregation concludes with vision, with their dream for the future.

"Only do not rebel against the Lord; and do not fear the people of the land, for they shall be our prey. Their protection has been removed from them, and the Lord is with us; do not fear them." (v. 9)

But so sharp is the division between the ten and the two that the majority seeks to forever silence the minority report: "All the congregation said to stone them with stones" (v. 10a). However, the Lord intervenes in judgment against the majority.

Then the glory of the Lord appeared in the tent of meeting to all the sons of Israel. And the Lord said to Moses, "How long will this people spurn Me? And how long will they not believe in Me, despite all the signs which I have performed in their midst? I will smite them with pestilence and dispossess them, and I will make you into a nation greater and mightier than they." (vv. 10b–12)

In turn, Moses intercedes on behalf of the people in order to save the Lord's shining reputation from any possible tarnish before the eyes of the world.

But Moses said to the Lord, "Then the Egyptians will hear of it, for by Thy strength Thou didst bring up this people from their midst, and they will tell it to the inhabitants of this land. They have heard that Thou, O Lord, art in the midst of this people, for Thou, O Lord, art seen eye to eye, while Thy cloud stands over them; and Thou dost go before them in a pillar of cloud by day and in a pillar of fire by night. Now if Thou dost slay this people as one man, then the nations who have heard of Thy fame will say, 'Because the Lord could not bring this people into the land which He promised them by oath, therefore He slaughtered them in the wilderness.' But now, I pray, let the power of the Lord be great, just as Thou hast declared, 'The Lord is slow to anger and abundant in lovingkindness, forgiving iniquity and transgression; but He will by no means clear the guilty, visiting the iniquity of the fathers on the children to the third and the fourth generations.' Pardon, I pray, the iniquity of this people according to the greatness of Thy lovingkindness, just as Thou also hast forgiven this people, from Egypt even until now." (vv. 13–19)

Moses' pure appeal sheathed the sharp sword of God's impending judgment (vv. 20–24). Yet, although God delayed immediate judgment, He caused the Israelites to wander in the wilderness for forty more years before entering the Promised Land—and ultimately, everyone who sided with the majority report died during that time (vv. 27–29). Ironically, the two who were to be stoned by the majority were the only men saved by God. Of the original adult population, only Joshua and Caleb were allowed to enter the Promised Land (vv. 30–35).

B. During the fight. Turn the pages of Israel's history forward to the book of Joshua. Here we'll see how Caleb and Joshua fared during the fight with the Canaanites. As we cross the threshold of this book, we leave the old, rebellious generation behind, buried in the wilderness. The new generation has invaded the land and fought their way to victory. And, just as He promised, God has given it to them. As we come to chapter 14, the land is about to be doled out among the twelve tribes. When it is Caleb's turn to choose his parcel, he stands tall and delivers one of the most determined, visionary speeches in all of Scripture.

> "I was forty years old when Moses the servant of the Lord sent me from Kadesh-barnea to spy out the land, and I brought word back to him as it was in my heart. Nevertheless my brethren who went up with me made the heart of the people melt with fear; but I followed the Lord my God fully. So Moses swore on that day, saying, 'Surely the land on which your foot has trodden shall be an inheritance to you and to your children forever, because you have followed the Lord my God fully.' And now behold, the Lord has let me live, just as He spoke, these forty-five years, from the time that the Lord spoke this word to Moses, when Israel walked in the wilderness; and now behold, I am eighty-five years old today. I am still as strong today as I was in the day Moses sent me; as my strength was then, so my strength is now, for war and for going out and coming in. Now then, give me this hill country about which the Lord spoke on that day, for you heard on that day that Anakim were there, with great fortified cities; perhaps the Lord will be with me, and I shall drive them out as the Lord has spoken." (vv. 7–12)

When most men his age would be looking to check into a sedate retirement village, Caleb was looking for new mountains—not only to climb, but to conquer!

At seventy-one, Golda Meir became prime minister of Israel. At eighty-one, Benjamin Franklin helped frame the United States Constitution. At eighty-five, Caleb rolled up his sleeves to take on the giants.

Age has nothing to do with vision, determination, or dreams. It's *what* you do, not *when* you do it. Remember that the next time you're tempted to use your age as an excuse.

So much for Caleb. What about Joshua, the other half of this determined duo? Page forward to chapter 23, and we'll find Joshua's determination intact.

"Be very firm, then, to keep and do all that is written in the book of the law of Moses, so that you may not turn aside from it to the right hand or to the left, in order that you may not associate with these nations, these which remain among you, or mention the name of their gods, or make anyone swear by them, or serve them, or bow down to them." (vv. 6–7)

Unimpeded vision. Undaunted dreams. Joshua stands in his senior years as an inspiring example.

"Now, therefore, fear the Lord and serve Him in sincerity and truth; and put away the gods which your fathers served beyond the River and in Egypt, and serve the Lord. And if it is disagreeable in your sight to serve the Lord, choose for yourselves today whom you will serve: whether the gods which your fathers served which were beyond the River, or the gods of the Amorites in whose land you are living; but as for me and my house, we will serve the Lord." (24:14–15)

III. Observations Worth Remembering

Three important observations stand out as we come to the end of this study.

A. **Age has little to do with achievement and nothing to do with commitment.** Both Joshua and Caleb were young men when they stood alone before their peers. Yet when they grew older, they were still standing strong, persistent in their convictions. The ranks of humanity are full of those who start well. With determination and persistence, you can also end well.

B. **A godly life is basic to a positive outlook.** Joshua and Caleb kept reiterating their full, firm commitment to the Lord. This commitment gave them a positive outlook in the face of incredible challenges. Without divine perspective, it's easy for negativism and cynicism to creep in. Do you want to maintain a positive outlook throughout your life? Then keep the Lord as the nucleus of your motivation.

C. Convictions are a matter of choice, not coercion. In their younger years, Joshua and Caleb stood alone against a nation; in their latter years, they maintained their convictions. They stood alone and served, not by coercion, but by choice. May their example encourage you not to take your cues from the crowd.

Living Insights

Study One ▪▬▬▬▬▬▬▬▬▬▬▬▬▬▬▬▬▬▬▬▬▬▬▬▬▬▬

Determination and persistence have separated the men from the boys throughout history. The Bible underscores this fact with a wealth of illustrations. Let's pursue one of these illustrations a little further—the story of Joshua and Caleb.

● Our study centered on three chapters of Joshua—14, 23, and 24. To gain a fresh view of the text, try reading these three chapters in a different version of the Bible, perhaps a paraphrase or alternate translation. When you finish, jot down what you've learned about determination from Joshua and Caleb.

Determination

_____

_____

_____

_____

_____

_____

_____

_____

_____

_____

Continued on next page

Living Insights

Think of the people who know you best—your family, friends, or co-workers. Would they characterize you as a person of determination? Spend a few moments pondering three "nevers." What is your response to these statements?

1. Never use age as an excuse for not getting a job done.

_____

_____

_____

_____

2. Never lose divine perspective.

_____

_____

_____

_____

3. Never take your cues from the crowd.

_____

_____

_____

_____

Priorities: Determining What Comes First

Matthew 6:33, Colossians 1:13–18, Luke 14:15–35

Robert Frost's poem "The Road Not Taken" describes two roads discovered during a walk in the woods. Frost knows he can only explore one, and he tells himself that someday he will travel the other. But, realistically, he knows he will never return. By the time we reach the end of the poem, we realize the poet is talking about something infinitely more important than a simple choice of paths.

> I shall be telling this with a sigh
> Somewhere ages and ages hence:
> Two roads diverged in a wood, and I—
> I took the one less traveled by,
> And that has made all the difference.[1]

No, Frost is not talking about the choice of paths in a wood, but the choice of paths in a person's life. Choosing a road symbolizes any choice we must make between alternatives that appear equally attractive but lead to entirely different destinations.

Whether you arrive at excellence or mediocrity depends upon the choices you make at the crossroads. And your priorities will function as signposts to help you determine which road you will travel.

I. A Reminder of Unseen Values

Priorities not only point the way, they also reveal the values that often hide beneath the surface of our lives. As the Israelites hesitated at a confusing crossroad, Joshua challenged them to make a choice. Then, charting the straight-and-narrow path to God, Joshua revealed his priorities and values:

> "And if it is disagreeable in your sight to serve the Lord, choose for yourselves today whom you will serve: whether the gods which your fathers served which were beyond the River, or the gods of the Amorites in whose land you are living; but as for me and my house, we will serve the Lord." (Josh. 24:15)

Joshua knew that service could not be rendered to two masters. Divided loyalties cannot maintain their balance for long. A shift in the center of gravity will always take place—our loyalties will always

---

1. Robert Frost, "The Road Not Taken." Copyright 1916, 1969 by Holt, Rinehart and Winston. Copyright 1944 by Robert Frost. Reprinted from *The Poetry of Robert Frost*, ed. Edward Connery Lathem by permission of Henry Holt and Co., as quoted by Laurence Perrine in *Literature: Structure, Sound, and Sense,* 2d ed. (New York, N.Y.: Harcourt Brace Jovanovich, 1974), p. 627.

lean toward one side or the other. This is precisely what Jesus tells us in the Sermon on the Mount.

"No one can serve two masters; for either he will hate the one and love the other, or he will hold to one and despise the other. You cannot serve God and mammon." (Matt. 6:24)

Because our master is God, Jesus exhorts us to let any concern for our provision fall on His shoulders rather than our own.

"For this reason I say to you, do not be anxious for your life, as to what you shall eat, or what you shall drink; nor for your body, as to what you shall put on. Is not life more than food, and the body than clothing?" (v. 25)

Jesus concludes by showing us our master's benevolence and how that should affect the way we order our priorities.

"For all these things the Gentiles eagerly seek;[2] for your heavenly Father knows that you need all these things. But seek first His kingdom and His righteousness; and all these things shall be added to you." (vv. 32–33)

Who's Number One?

"We're number one!" is the competitive chant of every athletic team, every corporation, every nation. Even churches get into the cheerleading act when they tout Sunday school attendance, conversions, or a multiplicity of projects and programs.

Egoism is really at the root of our priorities, isn't it? It's difficult to put anything in front of *our* careers, *our* goals, *our* desires. It's difficult because, in reality, *we* are number one.

Now, that may be a hard pill to swallow, but if the diagnosis is correct, then for our own sakes we'd better just get a tall glass of water and gulp it down.

Who or what is number one in your life? Before you rattle off a papal list of priorities, be honest with yourself about what dominates your thoughts, your dreams, your ambitions, your finances, your time.

II. A Revelation of Absolute Authority

Logically, God should have first place in our lives, because He created us and is our absolute authority.

For He delivered us from the domain of darkness, and transferred us to the kingdom of His beloved Son, in whom we have redemption, the forgiveness of sins. And

---

2. The Greek word is *zēteō* and means "to search, to strive for, to desire strongly." The verb's action is continuous and implies "to keep on striving for, keep on searching after, keep on desiring."

He is the image of the invisible God, the first-born of all creation. For by Him all things were created, both in the heavens and on earth, visible and invisible, whether thrones or dominions or rulers or authorities—all things have been created by Him and for Him. And He is before all things, and in Him all things hold together. He is also head of the body, the church; and He is the beginning, the first-born from the dead; so that He Himself might come to have first place in everything. (Col. 1:13–18)

First place in everything. Everything? Everything! That's His proper place. That's what it means to have Jesus as Lord of your life. Does He have first place in everything in *your* life? If you're dating someone, does Jesus have first place in that relationship? Or is that relationship competing for your loyalty to the Savior and causing you to make moral compromises? If you're involved in a business, is Jesus chairman of the board? Or do economic considerations veto His principles? If you're a homemaker, is Jesus the person around whom you're making your home? Or is He low on your list of priorities, somewhere after grocery shopping and cleaning the kitchen?

III. A Response of Incredible Relevance

At a dinner party recorded in Luke 14:15–24, Jesus tells a parable about priorities.

"A certain man was giving a big dinner, and he invited many; and at the dinner hour he sent his slave to say to those who had been invited, 'Come; for everything is ready now.'" (vv. 16–17)

If the host in this parable had been important enough to those invited, they would have made his dinner a top priority. But because he was not first in their lives, other interests wrested their attention.

"But they all alike began to make excuses. The first one said to him, 'I have bought a piece of land and I need to go out and look at it; please consider me excused.' And another one said, 'I have bought five yoke of oxen, and I am going to try them out; please consider me excused.' And another one said, 'I have married a wife, and for that reason I cannot come.'" (vv. 18–20)

Property . . . possessions . . . passion. These priorities came first with the invited guests. Inherently, these things are not wrong. But they are designed to serve us, not rule us. When they are subservient to our love for the Lord, they're good. But as masters, they dominate our lesser priorities with an iron hand. As a result of the feeble R.S.V.P. attempts by his intended guests, the host sends out another invitation—this time to people who were willing to rearrange their priorities.

"And the slave came back and reported this to his master. Then the head of the household became angry and said to his slave, 'Go out at once into the streets and lanes of the city and bring in here the poor and crippled and blind and lame.' And the slave said, 'Master, what you commanded has been done, and still there is room.' And the master said to the slave, 'Go out into the highways and along the hedges, and compel them to come in, that my house may be filled. For I tell you, none of those men who were invited shall taste of my dinner.' " (vv. 21–24)

Contextually and historically, the parable refers to the gospel invitation that was refused by the Jews and was extended instead to the Gentiles. As such, it illustrates in story form the truth of John 1:11–12.

He came to His own, and those who were His own did not receive Him. But as many as received Him, to them He gave the right to become children of God, even to those who believe in His name.

But the parable of the slighted host applies to us today as well. If we're too preoccupied with other priorities, then we can hardly expect to enjoy the feast of fellowship He has offered to those who put Him first.

IV. A Review of Personal Priorities

In Luke 14:25–35, Jesus thins the multitudes with a short course on personal priorities. Placing Him first in their lives would preclude competition from any other loyalty. No relationship—however intimate—can compete with Christ for first place in our hearts.

"If anyone comes to Me, and does not hate his own father and mother and wife and children and brothers and sisters, yes, and even his own life, he cannot be My disciple." (v. 26)

And no possession—however prized—can come between you and the Lord.

"So therefore, no one of you can be My disciple who does not give up all his own possessions." (v. 33)

Following Christ means taking "the road less traveled"—and that road leads to Calvary.

"Whoever does not carry his own cross and come after Me cannot be My disciple." (v. 27)

In the final analysis, at every decision, two roads stretch before us—roads that intersect, but lead to totally different destinations. The popular one is the way of self . . . leading to the dense, entangling overgrowth of ego. The other is the way of the cross . . . the less-traveled path that leads to the green pastures of intimate fellowship with Christ. I hope our study has encouraged you to make Jesus the number one priority of your life. And I hope you will be able to say with a satisfied sigh somewhere ages and ages hence:

Two roads diverged in a wood, and I—
I took the one less traveled by,
And that has made all the difference.[3]

 ## Living Insights

Study One

Our priorities reveal what's important to us. Whatever or whoever is in first place—if it isn't Christ and His kingdom, it is in the wrong place. But how does this relate in a practical way to our walk with God? Much of it comes back to our relationship with His Word.

- How do you keep the Scriptures at your beck and call? The answer is simple . . . *memorize* them! This study included one of the most important passages in the Bible—Matthew 6:33. If you've never done so, memorize this verse today. If you already have, choose another one that is especially significant to you. The key to memory work is repetition. Read the verse aloud and write it out several times. You'll soon discover that the verse has become yours.

 ## Living Insights

Study Two

Wouldn't it be great to discuss our priorities with a professional priorities consultant? The good news is we *do* have a consultant. And He's available anytime, anywhere, with the best rates around.

- Spend some time talking with God about the things that are important to you. Are your priorities in the right order? Ask Him to help you rearrange them, if necessary, or ask Him to help you keep them in order. Listen for His direction and guidance, and thank Him for His interest in your life.

3. Frost, "The Road Not Taken," p. 627.

Accountability: Answering the Hard Questions

Romans 14:10–12, Hebrews 13:17, Galatians 6:1–2

Plato said in his work *Apology:* "The life which is unexamined is not worth living."[1] Self-examination is painful enough, let alone scrutiny by others. The reason is uncovered by the noted writer Samuel Coleridge.

> The most frequent impediment to men's turning the mind inward upon themselves is that they are afraid of what they shall find there. There is an aching hollowness in the bosom, a dark cold speck at the heart, an obscure and boding sense of something that must be kept *out of sight* of the conscience; some secret lodger, whom they can neither resolve to reject nor retain.[2]

However piercing, inspection by self, others, and God is the refining process through which our hearts are kept pure. David was known as a man after God's heart (Acts 13:22), not because he was perfect, but because he acknowledged God's diagnostic scrutiny—he was always willing to crawl onto the operating table for God's exploratory surgery. This was the redeeming characteristic of his life. Notice how he begins and ends this psalm:

> O Lord, Thou hast searched me and known me.
> Thou dost know when I sit down and when I rise up;
> Thou dost understand my thought from afar.
> Thou dost scrutinize my path and my lying down,
> And art intimately acquainted with all my ways.
> Even before there is a word on my tongue,
> Behold, O Lord, Thou dost know it all....
> Search me, O God, and know my heart;
> Try me and know my anxious thoughts;
> And see if there be any hurtful way in me,
> And lead me in the everlasting way. (Ps. 139:1–4, 23–24)

That's fiber-optic scrutiny. That's a man whose heart is laid bare before the master surgeon's knife. That, in a word, is *accountability*.

I. The Essence of Excellence

We, too, can model David's excellence before the Lord if we will cultivate four key qualities.

---

1. Plato, in *Bartlett's Familiar Quotations,* 14th ed. (Boston, Mass.: Little, Brown and Co., 1968), p. 93.

2. Samuel Coleridge, *Aids to Reflection,* as quoted in *Handbook of Preaching Resources from Literature,* ed. James D. Robertson (Grand Rapids, Mich.: Baker Book House, 1962), p. 189.

A. A review of three essentials. First, people who live above the level of mediocrity and impact others are people of *vision.* Vision is the ability to see above and beyond the majority—to be unimpressed by the statistics, unintimidated by the odds, and unhindered by the obstacles. Second, people who impact others model *determination.* Determination is nothing more than the bulldog tenacity to tough it out through thick or thin. It trudges onward, no matter how rigorous the road, how rough the rocks, how steep the slope, or how dangerous the drop-off. Third, those who bypass the highway of mediocrity for the less-traveled road to excellence are people with their *priorities* in proper perspective—people who place eternal price tags on all their relationships, work, and possessions.

B. A fourth essential. People who breathe the rare mountain air of excellence are those who have learned the wisdom of *accountability.* Accountability is trusting your life to a few carefully selected, loyal confidants who love you—confidants who have the right to examine, question, appraise, and give counsel. Like ropes for a mountain climber, these people hold your life in check and keep you from slipping precipitously to destruction. Accountability has four sister qualities:

   1. **Vulnerability—lowering your defensive walls, even if it means exposure to possible pain.**
   2. **Teachability—being willing to learn no matter how difficult the assignment.**
   3. **Availability—being on call night or day for God's purposes.**
   4. **Honesty—being open to the truth no matter how revealing.**

Ropes of Accountability

Proverbs warns us that "Pride goes before destruction, / And a haughty spirit before stumbling" (16:18).

Pride often accompanies a climb to the top. When we scale the peaks of personal, financial, or corporate success, pride stands there beside us, looking down on those we left behind—those panting at the tree line, blistered on the foothills, cowering in the valley.

When looking down on others with self-satisfied smugness, we can become careless in our footing and forget that a disastrous fall is only a step away. But if people who love us are anchoring our ascent, their ropes can keep us in check and prevent us from stumbling to destruction.

> As you're climbing toward excellence, remember the perils at the peaks—and remember to have people above and below you holding the ropes.

II. A Scriptural Analysis of Accountability

In our society, privacy is a perk that goes along with promotion. Lack of accountability is considered the height of success—it is achievement's carte blanche. Yet, unaccountability, whether it's in the Oval Office or in a country store, is unwise. And not only unwise, but unbiblical.

A. Biblical principles. There are three major principles in support of accountability.

1. Accountability to God is inevitable and inescapable. But you, why do you judge your brother? Or you again, why do you regard your brother with contempt? For we shall all stand before the judgment seat of God. For it is written,

> "As I live, says the Lord, every knee
> shall bow to Me,
> And every tongue shall give praise to
> God."

So then *each one of us* shall give account of himself to God. (Rom. 14:10–12, emphasis added)

Each of us will be held accountable to God not only for our actions but for every word as well.

> "The good man out of his good treasure brings forth what is good; and the evil man out of his evil treasure brings forth what is evil. And I say to you, that *every* careless word that men shall speak, they shall render account for it in the day of judgment." (Matt. 12:35–36, emphasis added)

2. Accountability to spiritual leaders is commanded by God and profitable to us. Most of us have no argument with being accountable to God—the all-knowing, all-wise, all-powerful. The rub occurs when the awesome task of keeping us in line is handed over to ordinary human beings. As Paul concludes 1 Corinthians, he exhorts the believers to be responsible to the church's leaders.

> Now I urge you, brethren (you know the household of Stephanas, that they were the first fruits of Achaia, and that they have devoted themselves for ministry to the saints), that you also be in subjection to such men and to everyone who helps in the work and labors. (16:15–16)

The rationale for such measures of accountability is found in Hebrews 13:17.

> Obey your leaders, and submit to them; for they keep watch over your souls, as those who will give an account. Let them do this with joy and not with grief, for this would be unprofitable for you.

As believers, we are not islands, not dots of humanity in some unconnected archipelago. We are part of a vast continent known as the Church. We need each other, decidedly—and sometimes desperately.

3. **Accountability to one another is helpful and healthy.** When a member of the Body of Christ is weak, the stronger members should be there to help build that person up.

> Now we who are strong ought to bear the weaknesses of those without strength and not just please ourselves. Let each of us please his neighbor for his good, to his edification. (Rom. 15:1–2)

When sin disjoints a member of the Body, those who are healthy are responsible to set the broken bone with a physician's firm but gentle touch.

> Brethren, even if a man is caught in any trespass, you who are spiritual, restore such a one in a spirit of gentleness; each one looking to yourself, lest you too be tempted. Bear one another's burdens, and thus fulfill the law of Christ. (Gal. 6:1–2)

Listening to Advice

For accountability to work, you must cultivate the skill of listening to the advice of others. This is not a time for the red flag of reaction, but for the white flag of surrender.

And remember, although some advice must be taken with a grain of salt, no advice is entirely worthless. Even a watch that won't run is right twice a day!

B. **Historical examples.** Let's take a quick safari through the Scriptures in order to find a few trophies of accountability to hang on our mental walls. Blazing Old Testament trails, we find Joseph accountable to Potiphar (Gen. 39); Saul to Samuel (1 Sam. 13); King David to the prophet Nathan (2 Sam. 12); Nehemiah, as cupbearer, to the king (Neh. 1–2); and Daniel to his peers and several kings (Dan. 6). Crossing the New Testament boundary, we find Jesus as the epitome of accountability (see John 16:28, 17:4; Heb. 5:8). Following His example, the disciples were accountable to Jesus and later to one another; John Mark was accountable to Paul and later to Barnabas; Paul and Barnabas, in turn, were accountable to the church at Antioch; and Timothy was accountable to Paul, his father in the faith. Of course, like a flat rock skipping across the water, we've barely touched the surface of scriptural examples.

C. Practical advantages. Proverbs itemizes for us the practical advantages of accountability.

   1. When we are accountable, we're less likely to stumble into a trap.

> Where there is no guidance, the people fall,
> But in abundance of counselors there is victory.
> (Prov. 11:14)
> The teaching of the wise is a fountain of life,
> To turn aside from the snares of death. (13:14)
> Poverty and shame will come to him who neglects discipline,
> But he who regards reproof will be honored. (v. 18)
> He who walks with wise men will be wise,
> But the companion of fools will suffer harm. (v. 20)
> He whose ear listens to the life-giving reproof
> Will dwell among the wise.
> He who neglects discipline despises himself,
> But he who listens to reproof acquires understanding.
> The fear of the Lord is the instruction for wisdom,
> And before honor comes humility. (15:31–33)

   2. When we are accountable, we are more likely to see the whole picture. Most of us go through life like a horse with blinders: we see the path directly before us but we're oblivious to the periphery. Friends to whom we're accountable not only remove our blinders to give us a more panoramic view, they also sharpen our vision so we can see our own blind spots.

> Iron sharpens iron,
> So one man sharpens another. (27:17)

   3. When we are accountable, we are not likely to get away with sinful and unwise actions.

> Faithful are the wounds of a friend,
> But deceitful are the kisses of an enemy. (v. 6)

In a nutshell, accountability should be based on caring relationships—with friends who know us well enough to tell us the truth and love us enough to tell it with their arms around our shoulders.

> **Friendship: The Foundation of Accountability**
> Oh, the comfort—the inexpressible com-
> fort of feeling safe with a person,
> Having neither to weigh thoughts,
> Nor measure words—but pouring them
> All right out—just as they are—
> Chaff and grain together—
> Certain that a faithful hand will
> Take and sift them—
> Keep what is worth keeping—
> And with the breath of kindness
> Blow the rest away.[3]

 *Living Insights*

Study One ▬▬▬▬▬▬▬▬▬▬▬▬▬▬▬▬▬▬▬▬▬▬▬▬

If we are going to live above the level of mediocrity, we must make sure we've firmly cemented in our minds and lives the principles we've studied. At the halfway point in this series, perhaps a midterm review is in order.

- Listed below are the titles of our first ten studies, with space provided for you to record the most meaningful *truth* you discovered from each. Feel free to use your Bible and this study guide as you review.

LIVING ABOVE THE LEVEL OF MEDIOCRITY

Confronting Mediocrity Takes Thinking Clearly

It Starts in Your Mind (Part One) _____

_____

_____

Continued on next page

---

3. Dinah Maria Mulock Craik, as quoted in *Handbook of Preaching Resources from Literature*, p. 71. An excellent book on building this type of friendship is *The Friendship Factor*, by Alan Loy McGinnis (Minneapolis, Minn.: Augsburg Publishing House, 1979).

It Starts in Your Mind (Part Two) _____

_____

_____

It Involves His Kingdom (Part One) _____

_____

_____

It Involves His Kingdom (Part Two) _____

_____

_____

It Costs Your Commitment _____

_____

_____

It Calls for Extravagant Love _____

_____

_____

Overcoming Mediocrity Means Living Differently

Vision: Seeing Beyond the Majority _____

_____

_____

Determination: Deciding to Hang Tough _____

_____

_____

Priorities: Determining What Comes First _____

_____

_____

Accountability: Answering the Hard Questions _____

_____

_____

Living Insights

Let's continue our review of the first half of this series by turning from doctrinal truths to their application.

- Below you see the same format as in our previous study. Review each lesson and look for the significant truths you *applied*—one from each. Jot them down in the space provided.

LIVING ABOVE THE LEVEL OF MEDIOCRITY

Confronting Mediocrity Takes Thinking Clearly

It Starts in Your Mind (Part One) _____

_____

_____

It Starts in Your Mind (Part Two) _____

_____

_____

It Involves His Kingdom (Part One) _____

_____

_____

It Involves His Kingdom (Part Two) _____

_____

_____

It Costs Your Commitment _____

_____

_____

It Calls for Extravagant Love _____

_____

_____

Continued on next page

Overcoming Mediocrity Means Living Differently

Vision: Seeing Beyond the Majority _____

_____

_____

Determination: Deciding to Hang Tough _____

_____

_____

Priorities: Determining What Comes First _____

_____

_____

Accountability: Answering the Hard Questions _____

_____

_____

Winning the Battle over Greed
Luke 12:13–34

In his classic work *The Decline and Fall of the Roman Empire,* Edward Gibbon noted: "Avarice is an insatiate and universal passion."[1]

His words echo the sentiments Solomon expressed in Ecclesiastes: "He who loves money will not be satisfied with money, nor he who loves abundance with its income. This too is vanity" (5:10).

The Greeks used an interesting word when referring to greed. It meant "a thirst for having more."[2] Picture a shipwrecked sailor on a life raft in the middle of an ocean. His terrible thirst impels him to drink the salt water, but it only makes him thirstier. This causes him to drink even more, which makes him thirstier still. He consumes more and more of the salty water . . . until, at last, he becomes sick and dies.

Greed is like that—unquenchable, insatiable. Luke 12 preserves a similar picture of greed, framed in a parable. A bottomless well of living water, Jesus' advice on avarice quenches the soul's innermost thirst.

I. Several Faces of Greed

Greed—an inordinate desire for more—is an untamed beast that claws and clutches in a craving thirst to possess. The word *enough* is not in this beast's vocabulary. A glutton, forever hungry, it can only cry out: "more . . . MORE . . . MORE!" Greed's hideous face wears many masks, the first of which is money.

A. Greed is an excessive motivation to have more money.
Like Dickens's Ebenezer Scrooge—"a squeezing, wrenching, grasping, scraping, clutching, covetous old sinner!"[3]—greed is a hoarding desire for money. It touches the Midas in us all and gilds our souls with brittle, suffocating gold leaf.

B. Greed is an excessive determination to own more things.
This second mask is material possessions—an obsessive compulsion for more clothes, bigger closets; more china, bigger cabinets; more cars, bigger garages; more furniture, bigger houses.

C. Greed is an excessive desire to become more famous, to make a name for oneself.
This third is the mask of fame. Greed covets the lifestyles of not only the rich but the famous as well. From Narcissus in Greek mythology to Norma Desmond

---

1. Edward Gibbon, as quoted in *Great Treasury of Western Thought,* ed. Mortimer J. Adler and Charles Van Doren (New York, N.Y.: R. R. Bowker Co., 1977), p. 299.

2. From the word *pleonexia,* translated "greed" in Luke 12:15.

3. Charles Dickens, *A Christmas Carol* (New York, N.Y.: Dial Books, 1983), p. 12.

in the film *Sunset Boulevard,* this face is constantly surrounding itself with the mirrors and memorabilia of ego.

D. Greed is an excessive need to gain more control. The fourth masquerade is manipulation. Always wanting to be coach instead of player . . . chairman of the board instead of stockholder . . . queen bee instead of drone. Rather than serve, greed seeks to be the one who is served, the one in control.

II. Greed Exposed and Denounced

Our Lord realizes the hold material things have on our hearts. Seventeen of His thirty-seven parables deal with possessions and our responsibility to use them wisely. Luke 12 contains one such parable.

A. The dialogue. The catalyst to the parable was the urgent imperative of a greedy man.

> And someone in the crowd said to Him, "Teacher, tell my brother to divide the family inheritance with me." But He said to him, "Man, who appointed Me a judge or arbiter over you?" (vv. 13–14)

Although Jesus refused to referee the man's family affairs, He used the intrusive request to introduce a short sermon. In doing so, Jesus expounded a principle which sounded a warning against our enemy, greed.

B. A principle. Notice that Jesus didn't address this principle to the man but to the crowd (compare *him* in v. 14 with *them* in v. 15).

> And He said to them, "Beware, and be on your guard against every form of greed; for not even when one has an abundance does his life consist of his possessions." (v. 15)

Jesus warned the crowd not to let the masqueraded faces of greed fool them into thinking that life can be reduced to a banker's balance sheet. To illustrate this principle, Jesus told a parable.

C. The parable.

> "The land of a certain rich man was very productive. And he began reasoning to himself, saying, 'What shall I do, since I have no place to store my crops?' And he said, 'This is what I will do: I will tear down my barns and build larger ones, and there I will store all my grain and my goods. And I will say to my soul, "Soul, you have many goods laid up for many years to come; take your ease, eat, drink and be merry." ' But God said to him, 'You fool! This very night your soul is required of you; and now who will own what you have prepared?' So is the man who lays up treasure for himself, and is not rich toward God." (vv. 16–21)

A bumper-crop harvest but a bankrupt heart. What went wrong? Where did this man's plow take a wrong turn?

1. **He didn't know himself.** This man put all his eggs in the basket of the here and now, only to have them broken in an upending brush with the hereafter. He was a man who really didn't know what satisfied his soul. He labored under the distortion that ultimate satisfaction in life is derived from the creature comforts of ease, epicurean delights, and entertainment. Yet what he didn't know was that, like the rippled image of the moon on a lake, these pleasures were only reflections of the much higher, brighter pleasure of God Himself. It is in the light of this greater pleasure that all our lesser pleasures find their illumination, as Solomon noted:

> There is nothing better for a man than to eat and drink and tell himself that his labor is good. This also I have seen, that it is from the hand of God. For who can eat and who can have enjoyment without Him? (Eccles. 2:24–25)

2. **He didn't care about other people.** The man's remarks are thoroughly and unashamedly full of himself. Count the *I*'s and *my*'s in the parable. A total of eleven! Sounds like the self-indulgence of Solomon in Ecclesiastes 2:1–11. Look at the parable again. Count the *they*'s, *them*'s, and *their*'s. Not one! Because this man didn't care about the they, them, and their; he cared only about the I, me, and my. Greed hides behind the mask of the first person pronoun.

3. **He didn't make room for God.** The man worried about not having adequate storage for his crops. What he should have worried about was that he had no room in his life for God. His silos were marked Grain Only; he had no space for spiritual things, no room in his heart for God.

D. **A series of truths.** On the basis of this story, Jesus presented what appears to be something of a *Reader's Digest* condensed version of the Sermon on the Mount.

> And He said to His disciples, "For this reason I say to you, do not be anxious for your life, as to what you shall eat; nor for your body, as to what you shall put on. For life is more than food, and the body than clothing. Consider the ravens, for they neither sow nor reap; and they have no storeroom nor barn; and yet God feeds them; how much more valuable you are than the birds! And which of you by being anxious can add a single cubit to his life's span? If then you cannot do even a very little thing, why are you anxious

about other matters? Consider the lilies, how they grow; they neither toil nor spin; but I tell you, even Solomon in all his glory did not clothe himself like one of these. But if God so arrays the grass in the field, which is alive today and tomorrow is thrown into the furnace, how much more will He clothe you, O men of little faith! And do not seek what you shall eat, and what you shall drink, and do not keep worrying. For all these things the nations of the world eagerly seek; but your Father knows that you need these things. But seek for His kingdom, and these things shall be added to you. Do not be afraid, little flock, for your Father has chosen gladly to give you the kingdom. Sell your possessions and give to charity; make yourselves purses which do not wear out, an unfailing treasure in heaven, where no thief comes near, nor moth destroys. For where your treasure is, there will your heart be also." (Luke 12:22–34)

From this homily on the heart, we can gather enough truth to fill four concluding baskets. First: Those who lose the battle with greed are characterized by anxiety and a pursuit of the temporal (vv. 22–23). Second: Those who win the battle over greed realize their value in God's sight and simply trust Him (vv. 24–31). Third: Overcoming greed requires deliberate and assertive action (vv. 32–33). Fourth: Real valuables are sealed in our hearts (v. 34).

Relaxing Greed's Grip

Does greed have you clutching for money . . . material possessions . . . fame . . . control? Like Jesus in Gethsemane, won't you loosen your grip on life and submit, empty-handed, to God's will? In raising your empty hands to God, you will find a fullness you never knew existed.

One by one He took them from me,
All the things I valued most,
Until I was empty-handed;
Every glittering toy was lost,

And I walked earth's highway, grieving,
In my rags and poverty.
Till I heard His voice inviting,
"Lift your empty hands to Me!"

So I turned my hands toward Heaven,
And He filled them with a store

Of His own transcendant riches
Till they could contain no more.

And at last I comprehended
With my stupid mind and dull,
That God COULD not pour His riches
Into hands already full![4]

Living Insights

Study One ▬▬▬▬▬▬▬▬▬▬▬▬▬▬▬▬▬▬▬▬▬▬▬▬▬▬▬

Greed wears many masks, displaying itself through desires for money, possessions, fame, and control. It is the enemy of faith. This lesson should aid our understanding of greed and help us bring it under submission. Let's press on in our attempt.

* As you look up the following references dealing with greed, write down your observations. What is God's Word teaching you?

Observations on Greed
Numbers 11:34

Continued on next page

4. Martha Snell Nicholson, "Treasures," in *Ivory Palaces* (Wilmington, Calif.: Martha Snell Nicholson, 1946), p. 67.

Psalm 10:3

Proverbs 11:6

Colossians 3:5

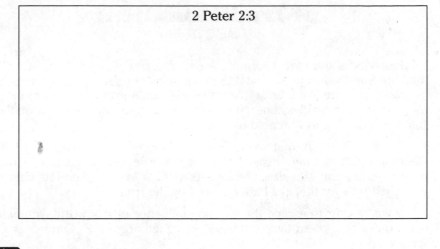

2 Peter 2:3

🐿️ *Living Insights*

Study Two ━━━━━━━━━━━━━━━━━━━━━━━━━━━━━━━━━━━━━━━

Did you realize that you could be greedy and not even know it? Many of us are blind to our own avaricious shortcomings. Here's a surefire method for detecting this weakness.

• Greed can be spotted by employing a principle we learned in our last lesson—accountability. Do you have someone to whom you can be accountable? Someone who knows you well enough to say the hard things to you? If so, ask this person to tell you about any greed showing up in your life. Many, many people benefit greatly from an accountable relationship. If you're not in such a relationship, begin right now by praying. Ask God to bring someone like this into your life. It's essential for your spiritual growth. And it's essential in your battle against mediocrity.

Slaying the Dragon
of Traditionalism
Luke 5:27–39

Passivity is the surest formula for mediocrity. Sit back complacently and the world will squeeze you into its mold faster than a waffle iron makes waffles (compare Rom. 12:2a). And like the waffle iron turns out monotonously uniform waffles, one after another, so the world mass-produces people according to the mold of mediocrity.

For the Christian, that waffle iron is traditionalism—rituals that have become rigidly set into a cast-iron matrix of rules and regulations. Traditionalism not only squeezes you into its mold, it forever leaves its imprint scorched on your life, like batter seared by the iron.

If you're ever to escape the molding influence of this world, you can't sit around in a room-temperature state of lethargy. E. E. Cummings expressed it well:

> To be nobody but yourself in a world which is doing its best, night and day, to make you everybody else, means to fight the hardest battle which any human being can fight; and never stop fighting.[1]

To combat mediocrity, a backbone has to emerge from the spineless batter of passivity. You have to stand up and resist. We're not talking cream puffs here. We're talking about a courageous knight who dons his armor, mounts his charger, takes up his shield, and brandishes his lance in a heroic quest to slay a dragon—the fire-breathing dragon of traditionalism.

I. Identifying the Dragon

Traditions, in and of themselves, are not bad. In fact, the right kind of traditions are good and healthy—traditions with a solid network of reliable truth that put us in touch with our roots. Paul exhorts us to "stand firm and hold to the traditions which you were taught" (2 Thess. 2:15). Conversely, he commands us to "keep aloof from every brother who leads an unruly life and not according to the tradition which you received from us" (3:6). However, a great deal of difference exists between *tradition* and *traditionalism*. Jaroslav Pelikan put his finger on the distinction when he observed:

> Tradition is the living faith of the dead, traditionalism is the dead faith of the living.[2]

1. E. E. Cummings, from a letter written in 1955, as quoted by Luci Swindoll in *You Bring the Confetti* (Waco, Tex.: Word Books, 1986), pp. 35–36.

2. Jaroslav Pelikan, *The Vindication of Tradition* (New Haven, Conn.: Yale University Press, 1984), p. 65.

By *traditionalism* we mean an attitude that resists change, adaptation, or alteration. It clutches tradition so tightly that the blood supply to our spiritual brains is cut off, distorting vision and blurring the distinction between custom and commandment. Traditionalism is suspicious and censorious of the new, the innovative, the different. It substitutes a stuffy, legalistic system for the Spirit's freedom and freshness; law for liberty; rules for renovation; regulations for renewal. In Mark 7, Jesus rebukes the Pharisees for confusing the custom of men with the command of God.

> And the Pharisees and some of the scribes gathered together around Him when they had come from Jerusalem, and had seen that some of His disciples were eating their bread with impure hands, that is, unwashed. (For the Pharisees and all the Jews do not eat unless they carefully wash their hands, thus observing the traditions of the elders; and when they come from the market place, they do not eat unless they cleanse themselves; and there are many other things which they have received in order to observe, such as the washing of cups and pitchers and copper pots.) And the Pharisees and the scribes asked Him, "Why do Your disciples not walk according to the tradition of the elders, but eat their bread with impure hands?" And He said to them, "Rightly did Isaiah prophesy of you hypocrites, as it is written,
>
> > 'This people honors Me with their lips,
> > But their heart is far away from Me.
> > But in vain do they worship Me,
> > Teaching as doctrines the precepts of men.'
>
> Neglecting the commandment of God, you hold to the tradition of men." (vv. 1–8)

Dirty Hands and Distant Hearts

By the time Christ appeared on the scene, the religious leaders had so tightly woven their customs into the fabric of Scripture that it was often difficult to extricate the truth of God from the tangle of human tradition.

But Christ cut through that tangle like a machete hacking through a jungle: God isn't interested in clean hands; He's interested in clean hearts (Mark 7:15). He isn't impressed with lip service (v. 6); He's impressed with obedience (vv. 9–13).

How about you? When you go to church, are you more concerned with the condition of your cashmere blazer than the condition of your heart? Are you more careful not to smear your lipstick than someone's reputation through gossip?

> Remember, God isn't concerned with outward appearances—He's concerned with the heart (1 Sam. 16:7).

II. First-Century Traditionalism

In Jesus' day the dragon of traditionalism reared its ugly head from the catacombs of Pharisaism—so much so that traditionalism and Pharisaism became virtually synonymous. In Luke 5, we see the Pharisees pressing their smug traditional noses against the dining-room windows of a tax-gatherer named Levi.

A. The parlor. Levi had apparently become a believer and left his lucrative job as a tax-collector to follow Christ (vv. 27–28). To introduce his friends to Jesus, Levi held an open-house reception.

> And Levi gave a big reception for Him in his house; and there was a great crowd of tax-gatherers and other people who were reclining at the table with them. And the Pharisees and their scribes began grumbling at His disciples, saying, "Why do you eat and drink with the tax-gatherers and sinners?" And Jesus answered and said to them, "It is not those who are well who need a physician, but those who are sick. I have not come to call the righteous but sinners to repentance." (vv. 29–32)

The indignation of the scribes and Pharisees gave Jesus an innovative opportunity to instruct—directly, with a principle; and indirectly, with a parable.

B. The principle. These formal stuffed shirts simply couldn't handle the festive freedom of Christ's disciples.

> And they said to Him, "The disciples of John often fast and offer prayers; the disciples of the Pharisees also do the same; but Yours eat and drink." (v. 33)

In responding, Jesus stated an important principle: *There's a time to fast and a time to feast.*

> And Jesus said to them, "You cannot make the attendants of the bridegroom fast while the bridegroom is with them, can you? But the days will come; and when the bridegroom is taken away from them, then they will fast in those days." (vv. 34–35)

As long as the bridegroom is present, it's time for merriment, not mourning. It's a time to celebrate ... to laugh ... to dance ... to sing ... to dine. Later on, when He's gone, that's the time to fast.

C. The parable. Jesus postscripted this principle with a parable—a parable that, like "Auld Lang Syne," rings out the old era and brings in the new. To do this, Jesus used two common word pictures.

1. **The new patch and the old garment.** The first illustration was homespun.

> "No one tears a piece from a new garment and puts it on an old garment; otherwise he will both tear the new, and the piece from the new will not match the old." (v. 36)

Anyone who grew up with unshrunk denim jeans and one-hundred-percent-cotton shirts can easily decipher this parable. Patch an old, shrunken garment with a new, unwashed piece of cloth and the patch will pull away from the garment when it's washed. Here, the old garments are the hand-me-downs of traditionalism. In an attempt to iron out the interpretation of God's Law, the Pharisees had added over six hundred new wrinkles. Like too much starch added to the wash, these rigid rules chafed the very people they sought to clothe.

2. **The new wines and the old wineskins.** Here Jesus changes to a more festive metaphor.

> "And no one puts new wine into old wineskins; otherwise the new wine will burst the skins, and it will be spilled out, and the skins will be ruined. But new wine must be put into fresh wineskins. And no one, after drinking old wine wishes for new; for he says, 'The old is good enough.'" (vv. 37–39)

If you take freshly made wine and pour it into an old, worn, brittle wineskin, you're in for a leaky surprise. It won't be long, thanks to the fermentation process, before chemical changes in the wine will cause the bag to stretch like a balloon and finally burst. The old, traditional skin of Judaism was simply too brittle for the new wine of God's kingdom that Jesus was offering. Judaism had become so inflexible that it was not a supple enough womb to give birth to this new era of God's grace. And so attached were the Jews to the wineskins of tradition that they actually preferred their stiff, empty wineskins to the full, festive truth of the gospel.

III. Twentieth-Century New-Wine Truths

Two significant applications jump out of the parable and hurdle the centuries. First: *Our God is a God of freshness and change.* Yet He Himself doesn't change (Heb. 13:8). His character is fixed, but His action is fluid—like a river flowing from a rock. Winding circuitously, the works of God wash freshly over both Testaments. The Old

Testament speaks of a new song . . . a new heart . . . a new spirit . . . a new covenant. The New Testament speaks of a new birth . . . a new creature . . . a new commandment . . . a new heaven and a new earth. The Bible's last reference to *new* is found in Revelation 21:5, where the Lord says that He's "making all things new." But traditionalism tends to resist the new and retreat to the old. Remember the bronze serpent God told Moses to hold up in the wilderness? It provided healing for those who were dying from snakebites (see Num. 21:8–9). For years the Israelites dragged that serpent around and revered it as a god. For years . . . until at last, God broke their tradition.

> [Hezekiah] removed the high places and broke down the
> sacred pillars and cut down the Asherah. He also broke
> in pieces the bronze serpent that Moses had made, for
> until those days the sons of Israel burned incense to it;
> and it was called Nehushtan. (2 Kings 18:4)

The second significant fact emerging from Luke 5 is: *New wineskins are essential, not optional.* Every generation has been tempted to restrict God's dealings. Most people are maintainers, not innovators. That's why traditionalism appeals to the majority. But in each age, new things are wrought by God. And if we're going to accommodate the new, fresh workings of God, then new wineskins are essential.

┌─ *Personalizing the Parable* ─────────────────────────────

Is your wine still fresh, or are you living on experiences from a generation ago? Are you tapping into new, bubbling, sparkling wine? Or has your faith grown flat and tasteless . . . lost its effervescence?

And how about the wineskin? Are you still flexible, or has traditionalism given your life a rigid, brittle texture? How open are you to change? How willing are you to risk? How quickly will you strike out in response to a new direction from God?

Living Insights

Study One ▬▬▬▬▬▬▬▬▬▬▬▬▬▬▬▬▬▬▬▬▬▬▬▬▬▬▬▬▬▬▬▬▬▬▬▬▬▬

The Word of God is timeless, containing truths that reach beyond all cultural confines. Nonetheless, certain activities and items are distinctly cultural in nature, as is this parable on wine and wineskins. Let's dig deeper into this issue.

● What role did wine play in the diet of those who lived in biblical times? Was it socially acceptable? Was it fermented? Is wine-drinking a cultural issue, or is it timeless? These questions don't have easy answers. One place to begin your research would be a good Bible dictionary. Look up *wine* and jot down your findings in the following space. For further study, use the bibliography provided at the end of most dictionary articles.

Wine in Biblical Times

_____

_____

_____

_____

_____

_____

_____

_____

_____

 Living Insights

Study Two ▬▬▬▬▬▬▬▬▬▬▬▬▬▬▬▬▬▬▬▬▬▬

From wine and wineskins we gleaned freshness and flexibility. Personally speaking, how are you doing in these two areas? Are your thoughts freshened by creativity? Are you flexible enough to be open, mobile, and willing to risk? Use the space provided to do a little assessing.

Slaying the Dragon of Traditionalism

What I'm Doing to Stay Fresh

_____

_____

_____

_____

_____

Continued on next page

What I'm Doing to Stay Flexible

_____

_____

_____

_____

_____

Removing the Blahs from Today
Psalm 90

Greek mythology records a story about a man with a terminal case of the blahs. His name is Sisyphus. Because Sisyphus had angered the gods, they had sentenced him to an eternity of meaningless labor in Hades. Once there, his onerous task was to repeatedly roll a rock up a hill, only to watch it always roll back down.

Homer, in *The Odyssey,* tells the story.

> "And I saw Sisyphus at his endless task raising his prodigious stone with both his hands. With hands and feet he tried to roll it up to the top of the hill, but always, just before he could roll it over on to the other side, its weight would be too much for him, and the pitiless stone would come thundering down again on to the plain. Then he would begin trying to push it up hill again, and the sweat ran off him and the steam rose after him."[1]

How would you like *his* job? Makes your case of the blahs seem like a vacation on the Riviera, doesn't it? This man could write the book on monotony. If you ever wanted a story on the wearisome routine of a meaningless life, Sisyphus would be the man to interview!

From time to time we all find ourselves pushing boulders uphill, only to have the burdensome things roll back down again . . . and again . . . and again. If we're not careful, we can get trapped in that meaningless valley, pushing monotonous boulders day in and day out. And before we know it, our lives add up to a lot of sweat and toil and monotony—with meaning evaporating like the steam from Sisyphus's back.

Our psalm for today will take us out of that valley and up to the peaks, opening our eyes to vistas we never knew existed.

I. Surveying the Psalm

Before we scan the exegetical horizon of Psalm 90, let's focus our binoculars on a few introductory matters.

A. The writer. The psalm's superscription reads "A Prayer of Moses the man of God." This is the only psalm attributed to Moses—a man whose life had great meaning but also great periods of monotony. From age forty to age eighty, Moses tended sheep in a desert. Try to imagine the monotony, listening to the same blah baas for forty years! The next forty he spent wandering in the wilderness with a larger, more headstrong flock—the

---

1. Homer, *The Odyssey,* in vol. 4 of *Great Books of the Western World,* ed. Robert Maynard Hutchins (Chicago, Ill.: Encyclopaedia Britannica, 1952), p. 248.

nation of Israel. Wandering in circles year after year . . . the same terrain . . . the same old food . . . the same stubborn people.

B. His style. The psalm takes the form of a prayer. Notice how Moses addresses God directly and personally in verses 1, 2, 3, 5, 8, and 13. His psalm begins on a high note, strikes somber chords in the middle stanzas, and then crescendos in an optimistic appeal to God.

C. An outline. The psalm begins with a strong emphasis on God in verses 1–2. With verse 3, the emphasis changes to man. The final verse brings the psalm full circle to "the Lord our God." Here we are reminded that God's favor in confirming our life and labor is the answer to our drudgery and doldrums. With this God/man/God structure, the psalm pictures the wheat and chaff of humanity held in the tender, cupped hands of the Almighty.

II. Breaking the Spell

Frequently, our boredom and blahs begin when we fall under monotony's spell. In this quasi-hypnotic state, we experience a spiritual vertigo that blurs everything. If we're not alert, we can be lulled into a stupor of suspended animation, and one day we'll awake to find ourselves yawning in the land of mediocrity. To avoid this, we need to select a reference point and fix our eyes on it until we regain our spiritual balance.

A. The right reference point. Notice how Moses establishes the right reference point in verse 1: "Lord, Thou hast been our dwelling place in all generations." Philosophers from Plato to Sartre have wrestled with the dilemma of meaning in the universe and have concluded: "A finite point has no meaning unless it has an infinite reference point."[2] For Moses, that infinite reference point was God.

B. The right perspective. Not only is the Lord "the God who is there,"[3] He is the God who is *eternal.* Eternity is the substance of life's shadows, and if we are to see our own lives in the right perspective, we must see them, as Moses saw his, in light of eternity.

> Before the mountains were born,
> Or Thou didst give birth to the earth and the world,
> Even from everlasting to everlasting, Thou art God.
> (v. 2)

2. Francis A. Schaeffer, *The Church at the End of the 20th Century* (Downers Grove, Ill.: InterVarsity Press, 1970), p. 10.

3. Francis Schaeffer, *The God Who Is There* (Chicago, Ill.: InterVarsity Press, 1968).

III. Probing the Soul

As we probe our souls during times of such philosophical wrestlings, three thoughts generally come to mind.

A. My life is so short. Moses begins his lament about life's brevity with an allusion to the curse that came from the Fall (Gen. 3:19).

> Thou dost turn man back into dust,
> And dost say, "Return, O children of men."
> For a thousand years in Thy sight
> Are like yesterday when it passes by,
> Or as a watch in the night.
> Thou has swept them away like a flood, they fall asleep;
> In the morning they are like grass which sprouts anew.
> In the morning it flourishes, and sprouts anew;
> Toward evening it fades, and withers away.
> (Ps. 90:3–6)

Notice the vivid word pictures: "yesterday"...a brief "watch in the night"[4] ... "a flood" ... "grass." Each image is so ephemeral, like watercolors paling against the canvas of eternity. As James says, we are "a vapor that appears for a little while and then vanishes away" (4:14b).

B. My sins are so obvious. A second thought usually lurks just around the corner when the blahs have got us down. We are overwhelmed not only by the brevity of life but also by the blatancy of our sins.

> For we have been consumed by Thine anger,
> And by Thy wrath we have been dismayed.
> Thou hast placed our iniquities before Thee,
> Our secret sins in the light of Thy presence.
> For all our days have declined in Thy fury;
> We have finished our years like a sigh.
> As for the days of our life, they contain seventy years,
> Or if due to strength, eighty years,
> Yet their pride is but labor and sorrow;
> For soon it is gone and we fly away.
> Who understands the power of Thine anger,
> And Thy fury, according to the fear that is due Thee?
> (Ps. 90:7–11)

---

4. In ancient times, the night was divided into three watches lasting four hours each, through which a person may have slept without even being aware of their passing (compare Exod. 14:24 and Judg. 7:19). Later, the night was divided into four watches lasting three hours each.

Remember the sin that haunted Moses throughout forty years in the desert—the murder of that Egyptian (Exod. 2:11–12)? After many regret-filled years of wandering, carrying the burden of not only his own sins but also those of the nation, no wonder his life winds down with a weary sigh.

C. **My days are so empty.** A third feeling often accompanies the blahs—the feeling that our lives lack meaning. We know our names are written in God's Book of Life, but we fear that we will be mentioned only in passing, like tombstones inscribed with names but no epitaphs. Moses gives us some valuable advice if we want our lives to be more than just footnotes on the pages of time.

So teach us to number our days,
That we may present to Thee a heart of wisdom.
(Ps. 90:12)

Psalm 39 expresses a similar plea.

"Lord, make me to know my end,
And what is the extent of my days,
Let me know how transient I am.
Behold, Thou hast made my days as handbreadths,
And my lifetime as nothing in Thy sight,
Surely every man at his best is a mere breath.
Surely every man walks about as a phantom;
Surely they make an uproar for nothing;
He amasses riches, and does not know who will
    gather them." (vv. 4–6)

Numbering Our Days

We live in deeds, not in years; in thoughts, not
    breaths;
In feelings, not in figures on a dial.
We should count time by heart-throbs. He most
    lives
Who thinks most, feels the noblest, acts the best.
And he whose heart beats quickest lives the
    longest.
Life's but a means unto an end; that end—God.[5]

IV. Singing the Song

In numbering his days—learning to live each day to the hilt for eternity—Moses breaks through the blahs. Like the birth of a fresh,

5. Philip James Bailey, *Festus,* as quoted in *Handbook of Preaching Resources from Literature,* ed. James D. Robertson (Grand Rapids, Mich.: Baker Book House, 1972), p. 111.

new day from the dark womb of night, a song of joy crowns Moses' mental labor.

> Do return, O Lord; how long will it be?
> And be sorry for Thy servants.
> O satisfy us in the morning with Thy lovingkindness,
> That we may sing for joy and be glad all our days.
> Make us glad according to the days Thou hast afflicted us,
> And the years we have seen evil.
> Let Thy work appear to Thy servants,
> And Thy majesty to their children.
> And let the favor of the Lord our God be upon us;
> And do confirm for us the work of our hands;
> Yes, confirm the work of our hands. (90:13–17)

In this psalm, Moses has written a lot about time and eternity and God's anger and His favor, subjects quite familiar to another psalmist—David.

> Sing praise to the Lord, you His godly ones,
> And give thanks to His holy name.
> For His anger is but for a moment,
> His favor is for a lifetime;
> Weeping may last for the night,
> But a shout of joy comes in the morning. (30:4–5)

Singing the Blahs Away

If you've been singing the blues about life, maybe it's time to change that old, tired tune. Why don't you sing a new song to the Lord ... even if you have to sing it in the rain!

Try singing a song like Moses'—a song of consecration that will help you wisely number your days according to the rhythm of eternity. Try taking to heart the words of the hymn "Take My Life and Let It Be," and sing them to the Lord.

> Take my life and let it be
> Consecrated, Lord, to Thee;
> Take my moments and my days,
> Let them flow in ceaseless praise.
>
> Take my hands and let them move
> At the impulse of Thy love;
> Take my feet and let them be
> Swift and beautiful for Thee.
>
> Take my voice and let me sing
> Always, only, for my King;
> Take my lips and let them be
> Filled with messages from Thee.

Take my silver and my gold,
Not a mite would I withhold;
Take my intellect and use
Ev'ry pow'r as Thou shalt choose.

Take my will and make it Thine,
It shall be no longer mine;
Take my heart, it is Thine own,
It shall be Thy royal throne.

Take my love, my Lord, I pour
At Thy feet its treasure store;
Take myself, and I will be
Ever, only, all, for Thee.[6]

 Living Insights

Study One ━━━━━━━━━━━━━━━━━━━━━━━━━━━━━━━━━━━

Did you realize that Moses was a songwriter? Perhaps he penned this psalm to fight off monotony!

• Psalm 90 paints a picture of contrasts. As the artist, Moses portrays God's power and man's frailty with masterful strokes. Read slowly through this psalm's seventeen verses and look for descriptions of God and of man. Record your observations in the following charts. When you have finished, write a one-sentence summary of your findings.

Descriptions of God	
Verses	Observations

6. Frances R. Havergal, "Take My Life and Let It Be," in *The Lutheran Hymnal* (St. Louis, Mo.: Concordia Publishing House, 1941), no. 400.

Descriptions of Man		
Verses	Observations	

Summary: _____

_____

_____

Living Insights

Any mother with preschoolers or summer vacationers knows the endless question: "Mom, what can I do now?" Boredom, monotony, weary routine...sameness lulls us, as well as children, into lethargy. Well, splash some water in your face, because we're going to launch an all-out attack on dullness! Answer the following questions to discover how you can defeat monotony.

● What circumstances typically cause you to feel bored?

1. _____

2. _____

3. _____

4. _____

5. _____

Continued on next page

93

- Is it possible for you to change these circumstances? _____
  If so, how will you start?

  1. _____

  2. _____

  3. _____

  4. _____

  5. _____

- Whether change is possible or not, how can God use these circumstances to give you added maturity?

  1. _____

  2. _____

  3. _____

  4. _____

  5. _____

Becoming a Model
of Unselfishness
2 Corinthians 9:6–7; Exodus 35:4–29, 36:2–7

Ebenezer Scrooge. The very name sounds stingy, doesn't it? Charles Dickens, in his classic *A Christmas Carol,* describes Scrooge as "hard and sharp as flint, from which no steel had ever struck out generous fire."[1]

Christmas Eve created for Scrooge a begrudged opportunity to show generosity toward one of his employees.

> "You'll want all day to-morrow, I suppose?" said Scrooge.
> "If quite convenient, sir."
> "It's not convenient," said Scrooge, "and it's not fair. If I was to stop half-a-crown for it, you'd think yourself ill used, I'll be bound?"
> The clerk smiled faintly.
> "And yet," said Scrooge, "you don't think *me* ill used, when I pay a day's wages for no work."
> The clerk observed that it was only once a year.
> "A poor excuse for picking a man's pocket every twenty-fifth of December!" said Scrooge, buttoning his great-coat to the chin. "But I suppose you must have the whole day. Be here all the earlier next morning!"
> The clerk promised that he would; and Scrooge walked out with a growl.[2]

Hardly a model of joyful generosity! Yet, in exaggerated form, Scrooge does model the attitude many people have toward giving today.

In this study, we will explore what it takes to break that mold—to become a true model of joyful generosity.

I. Mandate for Generosity
Right behind the gold medal of love shines the silver medal of joy (Gal. 5:22). And, like a medal, joy's reflection can hardly be hidden. Proverbs tells us: "A joyful heart makes a cheerful face" (15:13; compare v. 15, 17:22). Just as joy is reflected in our faces, it should also be reflected in our giving. The apostle Paul makes a profound statement to this effect in his second letter to the Corinthians.

> Now this I say, he who sows sparingly shall also reap sparingly; and he who sows bountifully shall also reap bountifully. Let each one do just as he has purposed in

1. Charles Dickens, *A Christmas Carol* (New York, N.Y.: Dial Books, 1983), p. 12.

2. Dickens, *A Christmas Carol,* pp. 21–22.

95

his heart; not grudgingly or under compulsion; for God loves a cheerful giver. (2 Cor. 9:6–7)

In the Greek text, *cheerful* is the first word in the sentence, thus establishing its emphasis in the author's mind. It comes from the Greek word *hilaros,* from which we get our word *hilarious.* It surfaces several times in the Septuagint, the Greek version of the Old Testament; however, this is the only place it appears in the New Testament. God prizes the hilarious giver—not the grumpy giver. It's not a matter of laughing all the way to the bank, but of laughing all the way to benevolence.

Scrooges in the Sanctuary?

Jesus told His disciples as He sent them on their first missionary journey: "Freely you received, freely give" (Matt. 10:8b). Could it be that we give grudgingly, like Scrooge, because we've never really come to grips with grace? Could it be that we have difficulty giving freely because we have never received freely?

II. Models of Generosity

Negative models like Scrooge are not enough to repel us from selfishness. We also need positive models to attract us to generosity.

A. From the Old Testament. We see a classic example of joyful generosity during the Israelites' sojourn in the wilderness. Here God gave them an architectural blueprint for a portable worship center (Exod. 25–31). In Exodus 35, Moses revealed God's fundraising plan for the proposed tabernacle—the contributions of the people (vv. 4–19)! The Israelites' response to this request was indeed heartwarming, as it came not from human coercion but from divine coaxing.

> Then all the congregation of the sons of Israel departed from Moses' presence. And everyone whose heart stirred him and everyone whose spirit moved him came and brought the Lord's contribution for the work of the tent of meeting and for all its service and for the holy garments. Then all whose hearts moved them, both men and women, came and brought brooches and earrings and signet rings and bracelets, all articles of gold; so did every man who presented an offering of gold to the Lord. . . . The Israelites, all the men and women, whose heart moved them to bring material for all the work, which the Lord had commanded through Moses to be done, brought a freewill offering to the Lord. (vv. 20–29)

The Spirit of God moved among the people in a mighty way. In a broad, sweeping gesture of generosity, the nation united around the common cause of constructing for God a dwelling place in their midst. So willing were the people to give of their resources that Moses finally had to stop the flood of offerings (36:2–7). What an incredible model of hilarious generosity! Another impressive Old Testament model can be found in the rebuilding of Jerusalem's walls during the time of Nehemiah (Neh. 2:17–18, 4:6, 6:15–16).

B. From the New Testament. Crossing the Old Testament's literary border into the pages of the New, we tiptoe into a reverent setting where the wise men are demonstrating joyful giving as they worship.

> And when they saw the star, they rejoiced exceedingly with great joy. And they came into the house and saw the Child with Mary His mother; and they fell down and worshiped Him; and opening their treasures they presented to Him gifts of gold and frankincense and myrrh. (Matt. 2:10–11)

What characterized their attitudes? Joy. Exceedingly great joy. The result? Generosity. Extravagant generosity. Joy's effervescence bubbles into all areas of our lives. When it touches our wallets, it overflows in extravagance. How extravagant is *your* giving? Does the clattering of collection plates cause you to cringe in your padded pew? Do your George Washingtons squint painfully when exposed to the light of day? If so, maybe you have more of a bah-humbug attitude than one of festive Christmas joy. The problem may be that rather than the Savior sitting on the throne of your life, there crouches the silhouette of Scrooge, hoarding your money . . . at your own expense.

III. Methods for Motivating Generosity

Turning from biblical models of magnanimity, let's give our attention to three methods for bringing joy and generosity back into our lives.

A. Reflect on God's gifts to you. In Psalm 103, David shows us how to meditate on God's blessings.

> Bless the Lord, O my soul;
> And all that is within me, bless His holy name.
> Bless the Lord, O my soul,
> And forget none of His benefits;
> Who pardons all your iniquities;
> Who heals all your diseases;
> Who redeems your life from the pit;
> Who crowns you with lovingkindness and compassion;

Who satisfies your years with good things,
So that your youth is renewed like the eagle. (vv. 1–5)
What iniquities of yours has God pardoned? From what diseases
has He healed you? From what pit has He rescued you? How
has He bestowed His love and kindness on you? All that we have
are gifts from God—eyesight ... memory ... skill ... money ...
family—gifts sourced in the hilarious generosity of God.

B. Remind yourself of His promises regarding generosity. If we sow bountifully, we shall reap bountifully (2 Cor. 9:6b).
The generous man will be prosperous,
And he who waters will himself be watered.
(Prov. 11:25)
"Give, and it will be given to you; good measure, pressed
down, shaken together, running over, they will pour
into your lap. For by your standard of measure it will
be measured to you in return." (Luke 6:38)

C. Examine your heart. Audit the ledger of your heart's motivations. Here are a couple of questions to get you started: Am I
giving out of guilt, or out of joy? Am I trying to please my peers
as they look over my shoulder, or am I trying to please God,
who sees in secret?

IV. A Majestic Model of Generosity

Sometimes we tend to picture God as a miserly old man, clutching
His wealth of blessings with a tight fist. Consequently, we pray as
though we're pleading for God to pry those blessings loose. Nothing
could be farther from the truth. John 3:16 cameos a more accurate
image of God.

God .... the greatest giver
so loved .... the greatest motive
the world .... the greatest need
that He gave .... the greatest act
His only begotten Son .... the greatest gift
that whoever .... the greatest invitation
believes in Him .... the greatest opportunity
should not perish .... the greatest deliverance
but have eternal life .... the greatest joy

From Penny-Pincher to Philanthropist

Despite his miserly beginnings, Ebenezer Scrooge had a
magnanimous ending. A changed man by virtue of several telling encounters, he came on Christmas Day to the home of his
employee Bob Cratchit ... to make amends.
"A merry Christmas, Bob!" said Scrooge, with
an earnestness that could not be mistaken, as he

clapped him on the back. "A merrier Christmas, Bob, my good fellow, than I have given you, for many a year! I'll raise your salary, and endeavour to assist your struggling family...."

Scrooge was better than his word. He did it all, and infinitely more.... He became as good a friend, as good a master, and as good a man, as the good old city knew; ... and it was always said of him, that he knew how to keep Christmas well.[3]

If Dickens could change Scrooge, certainly Jesus—the author of our faith—can change the most begrudging of us into joyful, hilarious givers.

 Living Insights

Study One ▬▬▬▬▬▬▬▬▬▬▬▬▬▬▬▬▬▬▬▬▬▬▬▬▬▬▬▬▬

A selfish Christian is a mediocre Christian. The Scripture passages in this lesson advise against this stingy attitude. Let's get a fresh look at the joy that we as believers have available to us.

- Glance back over the verses covered in this study. As we have suggested in past lessons, it often helps to reread passages in a less familiar version of the Bible. Choose any translation or paraphrase you find particularly helpful.

 Living Insights

Study Two ▬▬▬▬▬▬▬▬▬▬▬▬▬▬▬▬▬▬▬▬▬▬▬▬▬▬▬▬▬

Why are Christians so often glum? Where has our joy gone? Let's renew our joy in the Lord by singing to Him.

- Dust off the cover of your hymnal or chorus book and get ready to make some joyful noise! If you can, gather your family or friends to sing along with you. If that's not possible, sing joyfully all by yourself. It's amazing how songs release our pent-up emotions. If singing isn't your cup of tea, do something else joyful ... but do remember to do it, OK? Stop robbing yourself of all that God intends for you.

---

3. Dickens, *A Christmas Carol,* pp. 126–27.

Standing Alone When Outnumbered

Romans 12:1–2, Deuteronomy 6:10–15

"Remember the Alamo!" This cry has immortalized that famous Texas battle in our memories.

The siege on the San Antonio mission lasted from February 23 to March 6, 1836. Under General Santa Anna, 5,000 Mexican troops surrounded the Alamo and attacked it for thirteen days. Outnumbered almost 30 to 1, the Texas volunteers stood alone and fought valiantly. One by one, their ranks were thinned by the enemy's bullets and cannonballs. As the battle climaxed with a massive attack over the mission walls, all 182 men were killed.

The volunteers' strategy had been to delay the Mexican forces long enough for the Texas settlers to organize an army. And their supreme sacrifice did just that. A short time later, Texas troops under General Sam Houston mounted a surprise attack at San Jacinto, captured Santa Anna, and secured independence for Texas.[1]

Even though the battle of the Alamo was lost, the war for Texas independence was won—all because of a band of dedicated men who were not afraid to stand alone when outnumbered.

I. Standing Alone against the World

Standing alone is never easy. Yet we have the assurance that "if God is for us, who is against us?" (Rom. 8:31b). God plus one always equals a majority; and, though we may lose some of the battles in this life, we know that the war will ultimately be won in eternity. The world may storm our walls, but it can't conquer our souls.

A. The exhortation. In Romans 12:1–2, Paul urgently pleads with believers to break away from the herd instinct—to stand alone with God instead of following the majority.

> I urge you therefore, brethren, by the mercies of God, to present your bodies a living and holy sacrifice, acceptable to God, which is your spiritual service of worship. And do not be conformed to this world, but be transformed by the renewing of your mind, that you may prove what the will of God is, that which is good and acceptable and perfect.

Note that the passage is not referring to salvation —"brethren"; nor is it suggesting an optional course of action—"I urge you"; nor is it implying that it will be easy—"sacrifice." In his commentary on Romans, Donald Grey Barnhouse remarks on this passage:

---

1. See Lon Tinkle, *The Alamo* (New York, N.Y.: McGraw-Hill Book Co., 1958).

Not conformed, but transformed ... this is the life of the true believer in Christ. The first of these two words, *conformed,* is the translation of a Greek word in the New Testament and it means that we are not to go along with the world's schemes. The second of these words, *transformed,* is a Greek word which means a very radical change from one nature and life to another. It is the word *metamorphoomai* which has given us our word metamorphosis. When a tadpole is changed into a frog or when a grub becomes a butterfly, we speak of it as metamorphosis. There has been a marked and more or less abrupt change in the form and structure of the creature.[2]

B. The explanation. For the believer, that change isn't cosmetic surgery but radical reconstruction—from a human shaped by the world to one being conformed to God's image, which is Jesus Christ (Rom. 8:29, 1 John 3:2).

Radical Transformation

Consecrating our lives to Christ involves more than simply shedding our skin like a snake. It involves our complete metamorphosis.

Metamorphosis is seen most dramatically in beetles, butterflies, moths, flies, and wasps, where the larval stage differs greatly from the adult. This transformation occurs during the inactive pupal stage, in which the organs and tissues break down into liquid and are reorganized into an adult structure.

Are you dissatisfied with groveling in the world's dirt, worming around in your little vermicular routine? Do you want more than just a seasonal changing of skins? If God is going to transform your life, you'll have to crawl onto the altar. Before God can ever give you wings, He must dissolve your old self and restructure it according to His design.

II. Sizing Up the World's Mold

The Phillips translation of Romans 12:2 reads: "Don't let the world around you squeeze you into its own mold." The contours of the world's mold flow along the lines of fame, fortune, power, and money. If our inner convictions lie lumped in a pliable, amorphous mass,

---

2. Donald Grey Barnhouse, *God's Discipline* in *Exposition of Bible Doctrines,* vol. 4 (Grand Rapids, Mich.: William B. Eerdmans Publishing Co., 1964), p. 27.

we'll be shaped by our peers instead of by God. "Do not be deceived," Paul warns in 1 Corinthians 15:33, " 'Bad company corrupts good morals.' " The wisdom of Solomon reflects the same conclusion concerning the pervasive influence of our associates.

> He who walks with wise men will be wise,
> But the companion of fools will suffer harm. (Prov. 13:20)

The Age of Conformity

Dr. James Dobson, in his excellent book *Hide or Seek*, warns that adolescents are most vulnerable to peer pressure.

> The pressure to follow the whims of the group (called the herd instinct) is never so great as it is during the adolescent years. This drive may be all-consuming to a teen-ager when *any* deviation from the "in" behavior is a serious breach of etiquette. And there is tyranny in this pressure.... Each teen-ager knows that safety from ridicule can only be found by remaining precisely on the chalk line of prevailing opinion.[3]

With what kinds of friends do your children surround themselves? What kinds of books? What kinds of television shows and movies and music? These will all play a part in molding their lives. For better or for worse, they will leave their imprint.

III. Stampeded by the Herd

If you're following the herd, before you know it, you may find yourself caught up in a stampede, running with the crowd at breakneck speed. And if you're not careful, you may just find yourself plunging headlong off the side of a moral cliff. Moses warned the Israelites of just such a peril as they were about to enter the Promised Land, where they would encounter a wild herd of Canaanites.

> "Then it shall come about when the Lord your God brings you into the land which He swore to your fathers, Abraham, Isaac and Jacob, to give you, great and splendid cities which you did not build, and houses full of all good things which you did not fill, and hewn cisterns which you did not dig, vineyards and olive trees which you did not plant, and you shall eat and be satisfied, then watch yourself, lest you forget the Lord who brought you from the land of Egypt, out of the house of slavery. You shall fear only the Lord your God; and you shall worship Him, and swear by His name. You shall not follow other gods,

---

3. Dr. James Dobson, *Hide or Seek* (Old Tappan, N.J.: Fleming H. Revell Co., 1974), p. 116.

any of the gods of the peoples who surround you, for the Lord your God in the midst of you is a jealous God; otherwise the anger of the Lord your God will be kindled against you, and He will wipe you off the face of the earth." (Deut. 6:10–15)

Don't think for a moment that God doesn't care about the conduct of His children. Like a protective parent, He watches for dangers we are oblivious to. How easy it would be for the Israelites to follow the wrong role models. How easy it would be to forget who gave them the roof over their heads, the food on their plates, and the keys to their camels. Between the lines, Moses urges the adolescent nation to stand alone ... not to yield to peer pressure ... not to follow the pack.

IV. Standing against the Herd

Getting something for nothing breeds irresponsibility, which creates a careless attitude, which, in turn, can lead to a loss of standards. No illustration of this stands out so clearly as the generation that entered the Promised Land. They forgot their Father and succumbed to the pressure of their peers. How do we keep from forgetting God when the pressure of the world squeezes hard against our lives? In Deuteronomy 6:4–9, Moses gave the Israelites a string to tie around their mental fingers.

"Hear, O Israel! The Lord is our God, the Lord is one! And you shall love the Lord your God with all your heart and with all your soul and with all your might. And these words, which I am commanding you today, shall be on your heart; and you shall teach them diligently to your sons and shall talk of them when you sit in your house and when you walk by the way and when you lie down and when you rise up. And you shall bind them as a sign on your hand and they shall be as frontals on your forehead. And you shall write them on the doorposts of your house and on your gates."

Moses' advice is just as timely today. If we will take it to heart, it will help us remember God in our daily lives so that we will be able to stand alone—even when outnumbered by a herd of Canaanites!

Continued on next page

🌳 Living Insights

Let's do a little more study in Deuteronomy 6:10–15 with the purpose of personalizing this text.

• Paraphrase this passage by putting it in your own words. Try to capture the ideas and emotions that stand out to you.

My Paraphrase of Deuteronomy 6:10–15

_____

_____

_____

_____

_____

_____

_____

_____

🌳 Living Insights

Have you ever seriously considered how the world subtly squeezes you into its mold? The following four areas are contours of that mold, which make deep impressions on the clay of our lives. Jot down how your life has been impacted by each one.

• Fortune 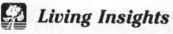_____

_____

_____

_____

- Fame _____
  _____
  _____
  _____

- Power _____
  _____
  _____
  _____

- Pleasure _____
  _____
  _____
  _____

Standing Tall When Tested
Judges 3:1–4

"Close your books. Put away your notes. Take out a pencil and a clean sheet of notebook paper . . . pop quiz!"

Bring back memories? Bad memories, most likely. Can you still feel a tremor of low-voltage terror at the mention of those words? Can you still hear your groans echo those of the rest of the class?

Pop quiz—probably the two words the average student fears most. Yet that method of testing is one of the most effective means teachers have of finding out exactly what their students know. God tests us in a similar way, but not to see what's in our brains . . . to see what's in our hearts.

In Genesis, God tests Abraham's faith with a pop quiz involving Isaac (22:1–19). In Deuteronomy, God hands Israel a forty-year wilderness quiz, testing them to find out what is in their hearts (8:2). And in Judges, after the Israelites have graduated from the wilderness and have been promoted into the Promised Land, God gives them another test.

Would they slump at their desks and fail the exam, or would they stand tall when tested?

Open your Bible to the book of Judges . . . get a pencil . . . a clean sheet of paper . . . and take notes as we find out how the Israelites scored.

I. The Test
Moses had prepared the Israelites for this quiz with a series of lectures recorded in Deuteronomy and handed down through the generations.

> "You shall fear only the Lord your God; and you shall worship Him, and swear by His name. You shall not follow other gods, any of the gods of the peoples who surround you, for the Lord your God in the midst of you is a jealous God; otherwise the anger of the Lord your God will be kindled against you, and He will wipe you off the face of the earth." (6:13–15)

Once they entered the Promised Land, it was time to close the books, put away the notes, take out pencil and paper, and start the new test. Referring to the nations that surrounded Israel, Judges 3:4 states the test's educational objectives:

> And they were for testing Israel, to find out if they would obey the commandments of the Lord, which He had commanded their fathers through Moses.

A. Their situation. First, *the Israelites were alone and uncertain.* Like timid freshmen on the first day of high school, they wandered

106

around the halls, sizing up their situation. And it didn't look good.

> Now it came about after the death of Joshua that the sons of Israel inquired of the Lord, saying, "Who shall go up first for us against the Canaanites, to fight against them?" And the Lord said, "Judah shall go up; behold, I have given the land into his hand." Then Judah said to Simeon his brother, "Come up with me into the territory allotted me, that we may fight against the Canaanites; and I in turn will go with you into the territory allotted you." So Simeon went with him. (Judg. 1:1–3)

Second, *they were inexperienced and vulnerable.* The generation that now found itself in the Promised Land apparently had failed to get its parents' notes from Moses' lectures.

> And all that generation also were gathered to their fathers; and there arose another generation after them who did not know the Lord, nor yet the work which He had done for Israel. (2:10)

Something vital is lost when a nation becomes severed from its historical and spiritual roots. Its strength of character is sapped. Its will to fight to preserve its heritage withers.

Prepared for Life

Whether the second generation cut class or their parents dropped the ball tutoring them (compare Deut. 6:4–9), the results are clear—they were not prepared for the test God had prepared.

Home holds the undergraduate degree that is the prerequisite for the Master's program of life. As parents, how well are you preparing your children for the pop quizzes and midterms in God's curriculum?

There's a third characteristic we must not overlook: *they were surrounded and outnumbered.*

> Now these are the nations which the Lord left, to test Israel by them . . . : the five lords of the Philistines and all the Canaanites and the Sidonians and the Hivites who lived in Mount Lebanon, from Mount Baal-hermon as far as Lebo-hamath. And they were for testing Israel, to find out if they would obey the commandments of the Lord, which He had commanded their fathers through Moses. And the sons of Israel lived among the Canaanites, the Hittites, the

Amorites, the Perizzites, the Hivites, and the Jebusites. (Judg. 3:1–5)

Archaeology has uncovered something about the culture that surrounded the Israelites at the time. The Ugaritic epic literature of the ancient Semites reveals the depth of depravity that characterized the Canaanite religion in their worship of numerous gods, including El, Baal, Anath, Astarte, and Asherah. "The brutality, lust and abandon of Canaanite mythology is far worse than elsewhere in the Near East at the time."[1] Hebrew scholar Leah Bronner notes:

> The gods themselves indulge in all pleasures, eating, drinking, and lovemaking, and perpetrate some of the most abominable deeds. They lived immoral lives, hated, warred, and killed often only for fun. . . . It is these lascivious practices, such as bestiality, temple prostitution, and child sacrifice, that are associated with Baal, which evoked the bitter invective of the prophets against the sensual Canaanite cult.[2]

Cramming for the Quiz

Things don't look good for the freshman class at Canaanite High. They are alone and uncertain, inexperienced and vulnerable, surrounded and outnumbered.

Have you ever felt like these second-generation Israelites? You may not benefit much from last-minute cramming for the test you're taking now, but it wouldn't hurt to crack open the Book and review God's educational objectives for testing:

> Consider it all joy, my brethren, when you encounter various trials, knowing that the testing of your faith produces endurance. And let endurance have its perfect result, that you may be perfect and complete, lacking in nothing. (James 1:2–4)

B. Their reaction. The first thing we notice about the Israelites' reaction to the test is *a lack of total obedience.* The Lord had issued His battle strategy in Deuteronomy 7:1–2:

> "When the Lord your God shall bring you into the land where you are entering to possess it, and shall clear

1. Merrill F. Unger, *Archaeology and the Old Testament* (Grand Rapids, Mich.: Zondervan Publishing House, 1954), p. 175.

2. Leah Bronner, *Biblical Personalities and Archaeology* (Jerusalem, Israel: Keter Publishing House Jerusalem, 1974), p. 84.

> away many nations before you, ... then you shall ut-
> terly destroy them. You shall make no covenant with
> them and show no favor to them."

However, as the grade book of Judges 1:19 records, the class fell short of a perfect score.

> Now the Lord was with Judah, and they took posses-
> sion of the hill country; but they could not drive out
> the inhabitants of the valley.

And the test scores only got worse—

> But the sons of Benjamin did not drive out the Jebu-
> sites who lived in Jerusalem; so the Jebusites have
> lived with the sons of Benjamin in Jerusalem to this
> day. (v. 21)

And worse—

> But Manasseh did not take possession of Beth-shean
> and its villages, or Taanach and its villages, or the
> inhabitants of Dor and its villages, or the inhabitants
> of Ibleam and its villages, or the inhabitants of Me-
> giddo and its villages; so the Canaanites persisted in
> living in that land. (v. 27)

And worse—

> Naphtali did not drive out the inhabitants of Beth-
> shemesh, or the inhabitants of Beth-anath, but lived
> among the Canaanites, the inhabitants of the land;
> and the inhabitants of Beth-shemesh and Beth-anath
> became forced labor for them. (v. 33)

The second thing we notice about the reaction of Israel is that they suffered *a loss of spiritual distinction.* Because they lacked total obedience—deciding to coexist with the Canaanites instead of obliterating them from the land—the Israelites compromised their way to spiritual infidelity.

> Then the sons of Israel did evil in the sight of the
> Lord, and served the Baals, and they forsook the Lord,
> the God of their fathers, who had brought them out
> of the land of Egypt, and followed other gods from
> among the gods of the peoples who were around
> them, and bowed themselves down to them; thus
> they provoked the Lord to anger. (2:11–12)

Finally, there was *a loosening of marital restrictions.*

> And the sons of Israel lived among the Canaanites,
> the Hittites, the Amorites, the Perizzites, the Hivites,
> and the Jebusites; and they took their daughters for
> themselves as wives, and gave their own daughters
> to their sons, and served their gods. (3:5–6)

The nation drifted into the shallow, precarious harbor of inter-marriage between themselves and the Canaanites—a union explicitly forbidden by God (Deut. 7:3–4). And sure enough, before long, Israel was on the rocks in its relationship with the Lord.

> And the sons of Israel did what was evil in the sight of the Lord, and forgot the Lord their God, and served the Baals and the Asheroth. (Judg. 3:7)

II. The Homework

To keep ourselves from failing the same test, a little homework is in order. Take notes and file away the following principles.

A. Standing tall starts with the way we think. It's a mind-set, the way we think about God, ourselves, and others. And our mental lenses color the way we view the rest of life—school, dating, marriage, business, family.

B. Standing tall calls for strong discipline. This involves our will—disciplining our eyes, hands, feet, and tongue. Keeping a short leash on the areas where we are prone to wander goes a long way in keeping us on the straight-and-narrow path of obedience.

C. Standing tall limits our choice of personal friends. Hang around the wrong crowd in the halls and you'll be sitting in the back of the class, staying after school, and maybe flunking out of life altogether. Remember: "He who walks with wise men will be wise, / But the companion of fools will suffer harm" (Prov. 13:20). Not bad advice. Particularly if you want to graduate from life with honors!

Living Insights

Study One

Judges 1 and 2 present the historical background for the period when the Israelites were led by judges. Chapter 1 discusses this era's political climate; chapter 2, the spiritual climate. Understanding this background will shed light on the Israelites' activities.

- Read through Judges 1–2 and jot down observations that reveal the Israelites' political and spiritual setting.

Judges 1–2	
Political Setting	
Verses	Observations
Spiritual Setting	
Verses	Observations

Continued on next page

🦁 *Living Insights*

Let's look again at the principles we've learned for standing tall when tested and apply them to specific areas of our own lives.

- *Standing tall starts with the way we think.* Name three ways you can renew your mind in the upcoming days.

1. _____

2. _____

3. _____

- *Standing tall calls for strong discipline.* List some ways you can stop the enemy from gaining victory over your will.

1. _____

2. _____

3. _____

- *Standing tall limits our choice of personal friends.* Jot down the names of a few friends who influence you positively.

1. _____

2. _____

3. _____

Standing Firm When Discouraged

Judges 6:1–6, 12–16; 7:2–8:35

In the ancient Near East, rainwater was caught and stored in cisterns, or wells. Usually constructed in the shape of a bottle, cisterns had small, circular openings at the top and larger, spherical shapes below the surface of the ground.

Into such a well Jacob's jealous sons threw their brother Joseph, thinking the young boy was doomed to slow starvation (Gen. 37:18–24). The brothers then sat down to eat, refreshing and nourishing themselves in grassy, sunny comfort, while their brother was crying for mercy in a dark, dank pit.[1]

At some point, we will each experience the rejection, the isolation, the loneliness, the discouragement of the well. Joseph experienced these things through no fault of his own. In our story today, however, the entire nation of Israel was in a pit of their own making, placed there by the disciplinary hand of God. In Joseph's situation, God used a Midianite caravan to rescue him from the well. For Israel, God used a man named Gideon.

I. Getting into the Well of Discouragement

Gideon was a man who stood firm when discouraged. Against his culture, Gideon stood out like a bright star in a moonless night. But before we turn the telescope on his life, let's examine the dark sky of history which presented such a striking contrast.

A. Israel's historical state. During Gideon's time, no monarch ruled over Israel. The people had no one to give direction, no one to set the pace, no one to model the truth or give instruction in righteousness. Judges 21:25 describes the setting: "In those days . . . everyone did what was right in his own eyes." Situation ethics made up the moral climate of the day. It's no wonder that ethical judgments were weighed with a thumb on the scale. Judges 6:1 measures the loss of morality and its consequences:

Then the sons of Israel did what was evil in the sight of the Lord; and the Lord gave them into the hands of Midian seven years.

The Midianites devastated and demoralized the Israelites, degrading them to such an extent that they were forced to live like animals.

And the power of Midian prevailed against Israel. Because of Midian the sons of Israel made for themselves

---

1. The historical account does not mention Joseph's appeals for help, but twenty-one years later the brothers, remorseful at last, recall the incident: " 'Truly we are guilty concerning our brother, because we saw the distress of his soul when he pleaded with us, yet we would not listen' " (Gen. 42:21).

the dens which were in the mountains and the caves and the strongholds. For it was when Israel had sown, that the Midianites would come up with the Amalekites and the sons of the east and go against them. So they would camp against them and destroy the produce of the earth as far as Gaza, and leave no sustenance in Israel as well as no sheep, ox, or donkey. For they would come up with their livestock and their tents, they would come in like locusts for number, both they and their camels were innumerable; and they came into the land to devastate it. (6:2–5)

Already up to their armpits in attacking alligators, the Israelites now found themselves shoulder-deep in a swamp of discouragement.

So Israel was brought very low because of Midian, and the sons of Israel cried to the Lord. (6:6)

B. Israel's spiritual state. The spiritual condition of Israel at the time gives life to these words of Jesus: " 'No one can serve two masters; for either he will hate the one and love the other, or he will hold to one and despise the other' " (Matt. 6:24a). Israel initially thought détente was possible between the Lord and the gods of Canaan. What started out as peaceful coexistence inevitably led to compromise, and with compromise came a confusion of loyalties. Eventually, Israel's allegiance shifted. Judges 2:12 marks the beginning of this departure.

And they forsook the Lord, the God of their fathers, who had brought them out of the land of Egypt, and followed other gods from among the gods of the peoples who were around them, and bowed themselves down to them; thus they provoked the Lord to anger.

The result of God's anger? "Israel was brought very low" (6:6a). So low they had to look up to see the bottom. So low they had nowhere else to look but to God: "and the sons of Israel cried to the Lord" (v. 6).

A Well with a View

Have you ever known such deep discouragement? Have you ever felt as if you were dropped into a well of insurmountable circumstances and left there to die? Maybe you're at the bottom of such a well right now. If so, look up to the Lord, as the Israelites did, and cry out to Him for help.

114

I will lift up my eyes to the mountains;
From whence shall my help come?
My help comes from the Lord,
Who made heaven and earth.
He will not allow your foot to slip;
He who keeps you will not slumber.
Behold, He who keeps Israel
Will neither slumber nor sleep.
(Ps. 121:1–4)

II. Getting Out of the Well of Discouragement

Five principles emerge in the account of Israel's deliverance. Serving as ropes, they will rescue us from the depths of discouragement.

A. Openly acknowledge what caused your condition.

Through an unnamed prophet, God gave Israel a direct answer regarding what had caused them to fall into the well.

" 'And I said to you, "I am the Lord your God; you shall
' not fear the gods of the Amorites in whose land you
live. But you have not obeyed Me." ' " (Judg. 6:10)

In a word: disobedience. But in owning up to their sin, the Israelites took the first step toward climbing out of the well. However, not all who stumbled into that well were there because of disobedience. Gideon, for one, had followed the Lord and kept to the straight-and-narrow path of obedience. But doubts arose in his mind when he couldn't reconcile his circumstances with his faith.

Then Gideon said to [the angel of the Lord], "O my
lord, if the Lord is with us, why then has all this
happened to us? And where are all His miracles which
our fathers told us about, saying, 'Did not the Lord
bring us up from Egypt?' But now the Lord has aban-
doned us and given us into the hand of Midian." (v. 13)

With a mandate of hope, the Lord began to dispel Gideon's doubts and discouragement.[2]

And the Lord looked at him and said, "Go in this your
strength and deliver Israel from the hand of Midian.
Have I not sent you?" And he said to Him, "O Lord,
how shall I deliver Israel? Behold, my family is the
least in Manasseh, and I am the youngest in my

---

2. Yet we see in the well-known incident of Gideon's fleece that his doubt was not totally dispelled (vv. 36–40). Like Thomas, he apparently needed some visual form of confirmation of God's word before he could fully believe. Just as Christ did with Thomas, God met Gideon where he was and agreed to answer the request for tangible support.

father's house." But the Lord said to him, "Surely I
will be with you, and you shall defeat Midian as one
man." (vv. 14–16)

**B. Focus directly on the Lord, not on the odds against
you.** Responding with faith and commitment, Gideon built an
altar to dedicate himself to the task of delivering Israel (v. 24).
The next time we see Gideon, he is alone, outnumbered, and
opposed—in a discouraging situation, but standing firm, never-
theless (vv. 33–35).

C. Declare your allegiance publicly. When the Spirit of the
Lord came upon him, Gideon summoned the troops with a trumpet call (v. 34). God honored his public declaration of allegiance,
and the troops rallied behind him and fell in rank. Have you
made it known to others where you stand? The trumpet of your
testimony must be sounded if you are to gain any degree of
victory.

**D. Remember that God prefers to work through a rem-
nant.** God does His best work, it seems, when those who serve
Him are fewer than those against Him. Note His' rationale for
paring down the troops to fight the Midianites.

> And the Lord said to Gideon, "The people who are
> with you are too many for Me to give Midian into
> their hands, lest Israel become boastful, saying, 'My
> own power has delivered me.' " (7:2)

Bolt by bolt, God radically cut the fabric of Israel's army, until,
at last, only a three-hundred-man swatch remained (vv. 3–8). In
His divine stitch work, God prefers working with remnants. The
first church was led by a remnant of twelve, and the Reformation
was spearheaded by a scrap of pastors. Doubtless, the situation
you're in at school, at work, in your neighborhood, renders you,
too, a minority—and that can be discouraging if you're not
willing to stand firm.

E. Do not accept the glory after God uses your life. God
used Gideon in a miraculous way to deliver Israel from the
Midianites (vv. 9–25). Victorious, the Israelites experienced not
only peace but prosperity as well. For the first time in years,
they had roofs over their heads and food on their plates. To
express their gratitude, they offered Gideon the monarchy.

> Then the men of Israel said to Gideon, "Rule over us,
> both you and your son, also your son's son, for you
> have delivered us from the hand of Midian." (8:22)

It would have been so easy for the valiant warrior to ride the
wave of his military success to the lush shores of fame and
fortune. But examine his unselfish response.

"I will not rule over you, nor shall my son rule over you; the Lord shall rule over you." (v. 23)

The Eagle Eyes of Excellence

At any given time, we are choosing to focus on one of four things: our circumstances, others, ourselves, or the Lord.

When outnumbered, Gideon refused to focus on his circumstances. And when victorious against overwhelming odds, he refused to shine the spotlight on himself. Instead, he gave the glory to the Lord.

An eagle's eyes are amazingly keen. On a clear day, an eagle can spot a dead fish floating on the surface of a lake five miles away. That's focus! If we're ever to win the battle over discouragement, we have to develop spiritual eyesight with similar clarity and concentration—even if we're the only bird in the flock to have it.

Living Insights

Study One

Today Gideons are scarce, even rare, but God still prizes people who stand firm in the face of discouragement. If we want to fill that role, we should study the script of this story carefully.

- Read Judges 6–8 and put together a little biographical sketch of Gideon. Start by answering the following questions. You can then expand in any direction you want to pursue.

Gideon: Judges 6–8

Who? _____

_____

_____

What? _____

_____

_____

Where? _____

_____

_____

Continued on next page

117

When? _____

_____

_____

Why? _____

_____

_____

How? _____

_____

_____

Living Insights

God says, "I searched for a man among them who should . . . stand in the gap before Me . . . but I found no one" (Ezek. 22:30).

- Could you be the one for whom God searches? What keeps you from being someone who stands firm?

_____

_____

_____

_____

- Why is it so hard to find people to "stand in the gap"? List some reasons.

_____

_____

_____

_____

- Take some time to pray. Talk to God about your day, your life, your need for help in standing firm when times get discouraging.

Boats, Nets, Fish, and Faith

Luke 5:1–11

Grauman's Chinese Theater—probably the most famous motion picture theater in all the world. Ever since May 18, 1927, this renowned Hollywood cinema, now known as Mann's Chinese Theater, has hosted the film industry's greatest stars in their finest roles.

Since its debut, more than 150 film personalities have imbedded their footprints, handprints, signatures, and personal comments in the specially prepared concrete at the theater's entrance. From Abbott and Costello to Artoo-Detoo and C-3PO, this concrete has fixed celebrities in its firm, gray memory.

Similarly, there was a place in the memories of the disciples where Jesus made a permanent impression. A place where He put His hands and feet and words in the wet cement of their lives and made an imprint so deep and profound, it would forever mold their lives.

I. The Setting

The incident began on the damp sands of the Lake of Gennesaret,[1] where Simon, James, and John were cleaning their nets after a long night of unproductive fishing. For weeks the Galilean countryside had been humming with news of a budding new prophet on Israel's horizon: Jesus of Nazareth.

> And He came down to Capernaum, a city of Galilee. And He was teaching them on the Sabbath; and they were amazed at His teaching, for His message was with authority. (Luke 4:31–32)

Not only did Jesus' message have authority—it had power as well. The subsequent exorcism of a demon had arrested everyone's attention in a compelling display of that power (vv. 33–35).

> And amazement came upon them all, and they began discussing with one another saying, "What is this message? For with authority and power He commands the unclean spirits, and they come out." And the report about Him was getting out into every locality in the surrounding district. (vv. 36–37)

---

1. "The famous sheet of water in Galilee is called by three names—the Sea of Galilee, the Sea of Tiberias and the Lake of Gennesaret. It is thirteen miles long by eight miles wide. It lies in a dip in the earth's surface and is 680 feet below sea level. . . . Nowadays it is not very populous but in the days of Jesus it had nine townships clustered round its shores, none of fewer than 15,000 people.

"Gennesaret is really the name of the lovely plain on the west side of the lake, a most fertile piece of land." William Barclay, *The Daily Study Bible: The Gospel of Luke,* rev. ed. (Philadelphia, Pa: Westminster Press, 1975), p. 56.

As a result, the next morning was abuzz with a hive of people gathered around Jesus.

> Now it came about that while the multitude were pressing around Him and listening to the word of God, He was standing by the lake of Gennesaret; and He saw two boats lying at the edge of the lake; but the fishermen had gotten out of them, and were washing their nets. And He got into one of the boats, which was Simon's, and asked him to put out a little way from the land. And He sat down and began teaching the multitudes from the boat. (5:1–3)

Doubtless, the fishermen had heard Jesus speak before, and they, too, had been awed, not only by the persuasiveness of His preaching but also by the power of His presence. Now, as they hunched over their nets, picking them clean of the accumulated debris, Jesus' words penetrated their hearts, making permanent imprints.

II. The Catch

When Jesus asked Simon to position his boat a little way from shore, Simon and his fishing partners consented. In doing so, they became a captive audience—literally. At the conclusion of His sermon, Jesus planned an object lesson that would be so vivid the fishermen would never forget its significance.

> And when He had finished speaking, He said to Simon, "Put out into the deep water and let down your nets for a catch." (v. 4)

Simon Peter must have thought Jesus was venturing into waters over His head. After all, fishing was Peter's business, his life; and Jesus was . . . well . . . a preacher.

> And Simon answered and said, "Master, we worked hard all night and caught nothing, but at Your bidding I will let down the nets." (v. 5)

Peter knew the best fishing spots and the most favorable conditions for making a catch, but, out of respect for the one he knew as "Master," he did as he was asked. Little did he realize the extent of the Master's domain!

> And when they had done this, they enclosed a great quantity of fish; and their nets began to break; and they signaled to their partners in the other boat, for them to come and help them. And they came, and filled both of the boats, so that they began to sink. (vv. 6–7)

Peter suddenly realized that he stood in the presence of deity. This Jesus was not simply a preacher with the power to heal; He was Lord of the entire universe! The words that followed this recognition are reminiscent of the experiences of Abraham, Job, and Isaiah when they, too, stood before the awesome presence of God (Gen. 18:27, Job 42:5–6, Isa. 6:5).

> But when Simon Peter saw that, he fell down at Jesus' feet, saying, "Depart from me, for I am a sinful man, O Lord!" For amazement had seized him and all his companions because of the catch of fish which they had taken; and so also James and John, sons of Zebedee, who were partners with Simon. (Luke 5:8–10a)

III. The Objective

As the boats filled with fish, the fishermen's hearts filled with awe. Speechless, they were now primed for what was to prove a life-changing announcement.

> And Jesus said to Simon, "Do not fear, from now on you will be catching men."[2] (v. 10b)

Jesus wasn't giving these rough, seasoned fishermen a lesson in fishing; His objective was to change their profession—by changing their lives. And change their lives He did.

> And when they had brought their boats to land, they left everything and followed Him. (v. 11)

Everything? The biggest catch these fishermen had ever made? Their boats? Their nets? Their livelihood? Their homes? Their families? Everything. Without an over-the-shoulder glance. Without even a second thought (compare Luke 9:62).

IV. The Application

The lessons we can apply revolve around three pairs of verbs: *chooses* and *uses, moves* and *proves, conceals* and *reveals.*

A. Jesus chooses not to minister all alone. He deliberately involves others in His work. He could have rowed the boat and cast the net Himself, but instead, He included the disciples. He didn't want a boatload of spectators; He wanted workers accustomed to rolling up their sleeves, feeling the tug on the nets, and sweating side by side. When He recruited them, He didn't say, "Follow Me, and watch *Me* catch men." He announced, "*You* will be catching men." How about you? Excellence in the Christian life requires casting our nets into the sea of humanity. Mediocrity lies tanning on the beach, watching the fishing boats of others sail by.

B. Jesus uses the familiar to do the incredible. Boats, nets, fish—all quite routine for the fishermen. But it is in the grind of the everyday world where God reveals His glory. What

---

2. The Greek word *zōgreō* means to "catch alive." It appears only one other time in the New Testament, in 2 Timothy 2:26, describing a person "held captive" by the devil "to do his will." That snaring of humanity will continue until God's people cast their nets and bring those people into the boat of salvation.

is your world? What is familiar to you? What is your profession or craft? You will be amazed at how the Lord can use you in your sphere of influence to do an incredible work for Him . . . and bring excellence out of even meager and mediocre surroundings.

C. Jesus moves from the safety of the seen to make us trust Him through the risks of the unseen. Christ took the fishermen past the shallows and into the deep water to cast their nets. If God is calling you to launch a similar boat of faith and you're teetering on the brink of that decision, don't be afraid to venture out. The Master of the wind and waves is in the boat with you.

D. Jesus proves our potential by breaking our nets and filling our boats. The catch of fish in Luke 5 perfectly illustrates God's ability to "do exceeding abundantly beyond all that we ask or think" (Eph. 3:20). These fishermen had never had such a catch—a catch so great that their nets began to break and their boats began to sink. If you will lay your skepticism aside just long enough to lower your nets, God will amaze you with His ability to fill them.

E. Jesus conceals His surprises until we follow His leading. It was fairly routine for the fishermen to launch their boats and head toward the place where they would cast their nets. This time was no different. The water didn't glow . . . there wasn't a halo around the boat . . . the oars were just as heavy as ever. The surprise didn't come until they lowered their nets. And that is when Peter realized Jesus was more than just a powerful preacher—He was Lord. When was the last time God surprised you? When was the last time you took Him at His word and He almost broke your mental nets with a display of His lordship over this world . . . over circumstances . . . over people?

F. Jesus reveals His objective to those who are willing to relinquish their security. Only after the disciples gave up the safety of the shore did Jesus finally reveal His purpose: "from now on you will be catching men." If we are ever to live above the level of mediocrity, we can't be landlubbers hugging the shore. We have to launch out into sometimes deep waters . . . and that means more than dangling our ankles in the shallows. Mediocrity will bid us, like a seductive siren, to rest secure on the shore. But the pursuit of excellence calls us to set sail into the waters of faith.

🐎 Living Insights

The story we have been studying in Luke 5 actually occured; it is in no way to be interpreted as a parable. Yet, we have much to learn from this historical account. It shows us principles of how Jesus deals with His followers.

● Reread Luke 5:1–11. What principles can you glean from this account? Review the applications we discovered in the last section of our lesson. Can you think of more?

Luke 5:1–11	
Verses	Principles

Continued on next page

Verses	Principles

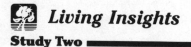 *Living Insights*

Study Two

Men and women of faith have many traits in common, not the least of which is a *closeness to God*.

- Let's use our Living Insights time to *pray*. Spend some moments in conversation with God, asking Him to forgive your shortcomings. Talk to Him about your strategy to be a real person of faith. Rely on His strength. Trust in His wisdom. Lean on Him. He will not let you down.

Standing Strong When Tempted

(Part One)

Judges 13:1–16:3

Goliath. Nine feet six inches of barbaric might and muscle (1 Sam. 17:4). A Philistine fighting machine, he waited in the valley of Elah to challenge the troops of Israel (vv. 8–11).

He stood in defiance, arrayed for battle, wearing a bronze helmet and clothed in scales of overlapping armor weighing more than a hundred pounds (v. 5). Bronze shin guards protected his legs, and a bronze javelin was slung between his shoulders (v. 6). He held a huge spear and had a shield so massive it had to be carried by his armor-bearer (v. 7). Only a small portion of his face was unprotected.

He seemed intimidatingly invincible.

Yet, in a confrontation with a young shepherd boy named David, Goliath would meet not only his match but also his demise. For a well-placed stone from David's slingshot struck the giant at his only point of vulnerability. And he fell, never to rise again.

Like the smooth stones in David's slingshot, the temptations of the world—fame, fortune, power, and pleasure—come at us with powerful force and hit us right between the eyes. These temptations are so direct and lethal that no giant, regardless of how spiritual, is invincible.

As we shall see in this study, one larger-than-life target of temptation was Samson. And the stone that brought about his fall was pleasure—specifically, sexual pleasure.

I. Samson's Favorable Circumstances

Few babies have come into the world swaddled with such favorable circumstances as Samson. Like John the Baptist and Jesus of Nazareth, his birth was divinely announced.

> And there was a certain man of Zorah, of the family of the Danites, whose name was Manoah; and his wife was barren and had borne no children. Then the angel of the Lord appeared to the woman, and said to her, "Behold now, you are barren and have borne no children, but you shall conceive and give birth to a son." (Judg. 13:2–3)

Furthermore, like John and Jesus, Samson was consecrated from birth.

> "For behold, you shall conceive and give birth to a son, and no razor shall come upon his head, for the boy shall be a Nazirite to God from the womb."[1] (v. 5a)

---

1. For the specifics of the Nazirite vow see Numbers 6:1–8. Essentially, Nazirites had to adhere to a strict diet with no strong drink; they could not cut their hair and could never go near a dead person.

And, like John and Jesus, Samson was given a unique life mission by God.

> "And he shall begin to deliver Israel from the hands of the
> Philistines." (v. 5b)

To guide him toward that mission, God placed Samson in the home of godly parents specifically chosen for their dedication and stewardship. When Samson's mother received the news that she was to have a child, she rushed to tell her husband, Manoah (vv. 6–7). Manoah wanted to understand his responsibility in raising this child—he wanted to prepare his son for his divinely appointed mission. So he entreated the Lord to send back the angelic messenger to teach him how to raise this child, and he listened intently to his instructions (vv. 8, 11–14). Samson's life was off to a great beginning before he ever left the starting block, for he had not only all these benefits but the blessing of God as well.

> Then the woman gave birth to a son and named him
> Samson; and the child grew up and the Lord blessed him.
> (v. 24)

Yet that solid start was no guarantee that he would accomplish his mission without breaking his stride. In fact, several hurdles appeared along the way to trip him up.

II. Samson's Flawed Character

The next time we see Samson, he is fully grown. We are not told about the first lap of his childhood, but it is apparent that his passion for God's mission has flagged. As he rounds the turn for the second lap, his spiritual flaws come into plain view—even from the grandstands.

A. Samson and the Philistine woman. Samson's lust lures him off the track, enticing him to refresh himself with the forbidden fruit of a Philistine woman.

> Then Samson went down to Timnah and saw a woman
> in Timnah, one of the daughters of the Philistines. So
> he came back and told his father and mother, "I saw
> a woman in Timnah, one of the daughters of the
> Philistines; now therefore, get her for me as a wife."
> Then his father and his mother said to him, "Is there
> no woman among the daughters of your relatives, or
> among all our people, that you go to take a wife from
> the uncircumcised Philistines?" But Samson said to
> his father, "Get her for me, for she looks good to me."
> (14:1–3)

Fixing his attention on the wrong objectives was what tripped Samson up. He focuses only on the woman's physical appearance and on pleasing himself. Twice we read in this account that the Philistine woman "looks good" to him (vv. 3, 7). He gives no thought to her character or even her name. Her sexual appeal is all that catches his eye.

> ### Samson's Snare
>
> It's important to understand some of the basic differences between men and women. Dr. James Dobson explains the sexual distinctions.
>
> > First, men are primarily excited by *visual* stimulation.... Women, by contrast, are much less visually oriented than men....Second (and much more important), men are not very discriminating in regard to the person living within an exciting body. A man can walk down a street and be stimulated by a scantily clad female who shimmies past him, even though he knows nothing about her personality or values or mental capabilities. He is attracted by the body itself.... Women are much more discriminating in their sexual interests. They less commonly become excited by observing a good-looking charmer...; rather, their desire is usually focused on a *particular* individual whom they respect and admire.... Obviously, there are exceptions to these characteristic desires, but the fact remains: sex for men is a more physical thing; sex for women is a deeply emotional experience.[2]

B. Samson and the Gaza harlot. Samson was drawn to the Philistine woman by his lust, but God used the match to strengthen Samson's foothold in that nation, helping to fulfill Samson's mission to deliver Israel from the Philistines (v. 4; compare 13:5). For twenty years Samson served as judge over Israel (Judg. 15:20), apparently ruling with faith and righteousness (Heb. 11:32–34). Again, however, his focus becomes diverted, and he is drawn off track.

> Now Samson went to Gaza and saw a harlot there, and went in to her. (Judg. 16:1)

C. S. Lewis summed up Samson's mistake when he wrote:

> The monstrosity of sexual intercourse outside marriage is that those who indulge in it are trying to isolate one kind of union (the sexual) from all the

---

2. James Dobson, *What Wives Wish Their Husbands Knew about Women* (Wheaton, Ill.: Tyndale House Publishers, 1975), pp. 114–16.

other kinds of union which were intended to go along with it and make up the total union. The Christian attitude does not mean that there is anything wrong about sexual pleasure, any more than about the pleasure of eating. It means that you must not isolate that pleasure and try to get it by itself, any more than you ought to try to get the pleasures of taste without swallowing and digesting, by chewing things and spitting them out again.[3]

Looking for Love in All the Wrong Places

Samson's preoccupation with physical pleasure eventually led to his demise. Our society shares his fascination—in fact, its gratification has virtually become a national pastime. Lewis marks this as a sign of a culture gone awry.

> There is nothing to be ashamed of in enjoying your food: there would be everything to be ahamed of if half the world made food the main interest of their lives and spent their time looking at pictures of food and dribbling and smacking their lips.[4]

What about you? What's the main interest, the primary preoccupation of your life? Is it the physical, or is it the eternal?

Samson's romp with the harlot nearly cost him his life (see 16:1–3; compare Prov. 6:26–28). Yet, as we will see in the next lesson, he jumps right out of the harlot's frying pan into Delilah's fire (v. 4). Each snare in this tragic hero's life is tripped by his sensuality, and, like the bird that "hastens to the snare" (Prov. 7:23), following after enticement did, finally, cost him his life. Samson serves as a graphic symbol of sensuality, and his illicit escapades vividly illustrate James 1:14–15: "But each one is tempted when he is carried away and enticed by his own lust. Then when lust has conceived, it gives birth to sin; and when sin is accomplished, it brings forth death."

3. C. S. Lewis, *Mere Christianity* (New York, N.Y.: Macmillan Publishing Co., 1952), p. 81.
4. C. S. Lewis, *Mere Christianity,* p. 77.

> ## Pleasure That Lasts
>
> "True pleasure consists in clear thoughts, sedate affections, sweet reflections—a mind even and stayed, true to its God and true to itself."[5]
>
> Finally, brethren, whatever is true, whatever is honorable, whatever is right, whatever is pure, whatever is lovely, whatever is of good repute, if there is any excellence and if anything worthy of praise, let your mind dwell on these things. (Phil. 4:8)

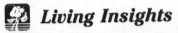

Living Insights

Study One

Before we continue our study of temptation, let's analyze the life of Samson. We can learn by his mistakes ... and, hopefully, avoid his pitfalls.

- In what settings was Samson tempted? How could he have avoided them? Where did he go wrong? Keeping these questions in mind, read Samson's story in Judges 13–16 and look for principles dealing with temptation.

Temptation: Judges 13–16	
Verses	Principles

Continued on next page

5. Hopkins, as quoted in *1,001 Sermon Illustrations and Quotations* (Grand Rapids, Mich.: Baker Book House, 1952), p. 85.

Verses	Principles

Living Insights

Study Two

Temptation is the most dangerous battle in the Christian life. Because of this, it would be worth our while to study it on a more personal level.

- Answer the following questions openly and honestly:

1. What area of your life poses the greatest threat in regard to temptation?

_____

_____

_____

_____

_____

2. In what setting does this temptation most often occur?

_____

_____

_____

_____

3. Which Scripture passages help you resist temptation?

_____

_____

_____

_____

4. Are you accountable to someone? Can you speak freely to a friend about your struggles? Why is this helpful?

_____

_____

_____

_____

5. Look at your circumstances from God's perspective. Does this make a difference? In what way?

_____

_____

_____

_____

• Talk to God about the temptations you face and ask for His strength to withstand them.

Standing Strong When Tempted
(Part Two)
Judges 16:4–31

Unlatch any fisherman's tackle box and you'll find a vast assortment of lures: shiny spinners with treble hooks, hand-tied flies, silver minnows made of balsa to float along the surface, weighted plastic worms with weedless hooks to wend their wiggly way along the bottom.

The goal of all this elaborate subterfuge is to entice some big fish into thinking the bait is dinner. But when the fish takes the bait, it isn't making a move on its next meal; it's making a move onto the next menu—as catch of the day! Whether artificial or real, bait is designed to appeal to the nature of the fish—to entice.

The word *entice* is found in James 1:14 in an image all fishermen can relate to: "But each one is tempted when he is carried away and enticed by his own lust." The Greek translation means "luring with bait," causing the picture of a fish to spring immediately to mind. As the fish meanders through the labyrinth of sunken tree limbs and underbrush, a silver minnow coyly shimmies by. Its scales catch a shaft of sun and send it glinting into the eyes of the waiting fish. That's all the enticement necessary. In a darting second, the fish clamps its cavernous jaws down on the minnow, only to be reeled into the fisherman's waiting net.

The account of Samson's temptation by Delilah also uses the word *entice* (Judg. 16:5). Like a hungry, unsuspecting fish, Samson is drawn out by the shimmy of Delilah's alluring appeal. Naively the bait is taken; fatefully the hook is set . . . and Samson ends up on a Philistine stringer.

I. The Unfortunate Example

As we saw in the previous lesson, few have grown up in circumstances as favorable as Samson's. His birth was divinely announced (13:3–5a), his life purpose was clearly spelled out (v. 5b), and his parents were deeply spiritual (vv. 8–12). Yet the negatives Samson welcomed into his life offset all the positives he was born with.

A. Unfavorable characteristics. Four negatives stand out in Samson's life regarding the man himself, his circumstances, his friends, and his spiritual commitment.

1. **He focused on the wrong objectives.** He concentrated only on physical appearance and pleasing himself (14:1–3, 7). He had 20/20 vision when judging a book's cover, but his reading skills were limited when it came to reviewing the book's contents.

2. **He handled his leisure time carelessly.** Samson's divinely appointed purpose in life was to "begin to deliver Israel"

(13:5b). Yet, he seemed to have a hard time staying on track. On a detour to visit this Philistine woman that had caught his eye, he took another side road and engaged in the trivial pursuit of propounding riddles while loitering around a Philistine camp (14:5–20). Samson had no business whiling away his time like this when the nation of Israel was desperately awaiting deliverance.

3. **He developed a close alliance with the wrong crowd.** Samson rubbed social shoulders with the very people he was supposed to subdue. In that crowd, he met Delilah— and made an alliance that would put him frying in a Philistine pan.

> After this it came about that he loved a woman in the valley of Sorek, whose name was Delilah. And the lords of the Philistines came up to her, and said to her, "Entice him, and see where his great strength lies and how we may overpower him that we may bind him to afflict him. Then we will each give you eleven hundred pieces of silver." (16:4–5)

In the words *entice him,* we see the chink in Samson's armor, which by now has become a gaping hole, obvious to all— even to his enemies. Delilah's weakness, however, is fortune, and she succumbs readily to its lure.

> So Delilah said to Samson, "Please tell me where your great strength is and how you may be bound to afflict you." (v. 6)

Amused, Samson dances to Delilah's seductive tune, teasing her frivolously at first (vv. 7–14), but giving in, fatally, in the end (vv. 15–21).

4. **He didn't take his vow seriously.** Frustrated with Samson for toying with her, Delilah nags him relentlessly to find the secret of his strength.

> Then she said to him, "How can you say, 'I love you,' when your heart is not with me? You have deceived me these three times and have not told me where your great strength is." And it came about when she pressed him daily with her words and urged him, that his soul was annoyed to death. So he told her all that was in his heart and said to her, "A razor has never come on my head, for I have been a Nazirite to God from my mother's womb. If I am shaved, then my strength will leave me and I shall become weak and be like any other man." (vv. 15–17)

This is probably the negative that offended God most—Samson's careless treatment of a sacred vow. Solomon, in his journal, addresses the seriousness of a vow made to God:

> Do not be hasty in word or impulsive in thought to bring up a matter in the presence of God. For God is in heaven and you are on the earth; therefore let your words be few.... When you make a vow to God, do not be late in paying it, for He takes no delight in fools. Pay what you vow! It is better that you should not vow than that you should vow and not pay. (Eccles. 5:2, 4–5)

Samson was taking the Lord for granted—perhaps because he had come to believe that his strength originated within himself rather than with God.

B. Inevitable consequences. Sin binds us and blinds us and becomes a demanding taskmaster, forcing our noses to a grindstone of harsh consequences.

> Delilah . . . called the lords of the Philistines, saying, "Come up once more, for he has told me all that is in his heart." Then the lords of the Philistines . . . brought the money in their hands. And she made him sleep on her knees, and called for a man and had him shave off the seven locks of his hair. Then she began to afflict him, and his strength left him. And she said, "The Philistines are upon you, Samson!" And he awoke from his sleep and said, "I will go out as at other times and shake myself free." But he did not know that the Lord had departed from him. Then the Philistines seized him and gouged out his eyes; and they brought him down to Gaza and bound him with bronze chains, and he was a grinder in the prison. (Judg. 16:18–21)

Like an eagle with a broken wing, Samson would never fly again. But he would make one last attempt to deliver Israel. This attempt, however, would cost him his life (vv. 22–31). Two inevitable consequences occur when we bite down on the alluring bait of temptation. First, we are weakened, not strengthened. Second, we become enslaved, not freed. The hook hidden in the bait has a merciless barb.

The Strangling Cords of Sin

Just as Gulliver was captured by the Lilliputians, so Samson, while sleeping, became entangled in the Philistines' cords.

> The man with great strength suddenly became weak.
> The man sent to bring victory was now the victim. Such
> are the inextricably binding effects of sin.
>
> > His own iniquities will capture the wicked,
> > And he will be held with the cords of his sin.
> > (Prov. 5:22)
>
> Is your sin like a tangle of fishing line . . . knotty, out of
> hand? If so, be careful—sin has a way of entwining itself
> around us, and what looks like lightweight line can turn
> into a boa constrictor, squeezing the life completely out
> of us.

II. The Victorious Strategy

To become victor instead of victim, we need to cut through the cords
of our sinful habits.

A. **We must counteract our natural focus.** We should focus
on "the hidden person of the heart" (1 Pet. 3:4) rather than on
externals (v. 3; compare 1 Sam. 16:7). How's your eyesight? Is it
sharpened with eternal perspective? Can you see beyond the
externals into the heart of another person?

B. **We must guard our leisure time.** Since the Devil never
takes weekends off, our spiritual life must stand sentry over our
pleasures and passions. Self-control is one of the fruits of the
Spirit (Gal. 5:22–23). Are you controlling your passions, especially during idle moments?

C. **We must screen our close companions.** Take a good
look at your circle of friends. Are they challenging you, or cor-
rupting you? Are they contributing to your spiritual dedication,
or to your delinquency?

D. **We must uphold our view of God.** Our commitment must
be taken seriously. For richer or for poorer, in sickness and in
health, for better or for worse, our commitment to God must
be steadfast. This is the only way we'll be able to stand strong
when tempted—the only way we'll have the strength to pass up
the tantalizing bait this world dangles in front of us.

Living Insights

We'd be doing a pretty mediocre job of discussing mediocrity if we didn't include a time of review. Sometimes more learning takes place during review than in the initial teaching situation. So let's see where we've been.

- Below are the lesson titles from the last half of our series. In the space provided, write the most meaningful *truth* you learned from each lesson. Go back through your study guide and Bible in order to make this an effective review. We'll talk about application in the next study.

LIVING ABOVE THE LEVEL OF MEDIOCRITY

Combating Mediocrity Requires Fighting Fiercely

Winning the Battle over Greed _____

_____

_____

Slaying the Dragon of Traditionalism _____

_____

_____

Removing the Blahs from Today _____

_____

_____

Becoming a Model of Unselfishness _____

_____

_____

Resisting Mediocrity Includes Standing Courageously

Standing Alone When Outnumbered _____

_____

_____

Standing Tall When Tested _____

_____

_____

Standing Firm When Discouraged _____

_____

_____

Boats, Nets, Fish, and Faith _____

_____

_____

Standing Strong When Tempted (Part One) _____

_____

_____

Standing Strong When Tempted (Part Two) _____

_____

_____

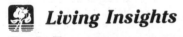 **Living Insights**

Study Two ▰▰▰▰▰▰▰▰▰▰▰▰▰▰▰▰▰▰▰▰▰▰▰▰▰▰▰▰▰▰▰▰

Let's continue our final review by turning our attention to the applications we've made. How has your life changed as a result of our time together? Are you learning how to live above the level of mediocrity?

- The following is similar to the one in the previous study. This time, however, go back through your Bible and study guide and look for an *application* from each lesson.

LIVING ABOVE THE LEVEL OF MEDIOCRITY

Combating Mediocrity Requires Fighting Fiercely

Winning the Battle over Greed _____

_____

_____

Continued on next page

Slaying the Dragon of Traditionalism _____

_____

_____

Removing the Blahs from Today _____

_____

_____

Becoming a Model of Unselfishness _____

_____

_____

Resisting Mediocrity Includes Standing Courageously

Standing Alone When Outnumbered _____

_____

_____

Standing Tall When Tested _____

_____

_____

Standing Firm When Discouraged _____

_____

_____

Boats, Nets, Fish, and Faith _____

_____

_____

Standing Strong When Tempted (Part One) _____

_____

_____

Standing Strong When Tempted (Part Two) _____

_____

_____

Books for Probing Further

Ted W. Engstrom, president of World Vision, retells a poignant story about mediocrity that serves as a modern parable.

An American Indian tells about a brave who found an eagle's egg and put it into the nest of a prairie chicken. The eaglet hatched with the brood of chicks and grew up with them.

All his life, the changeling eagle, thinking he was a prairie chicken, did what the prairie chickens did. He scratched in the dirt for seeds and insects to eat. He clucked and cackled. And he flew in a brief thrashing of wings and flurry of feathers no more than a few feet off the ground. After all, that's how prairie chickens were supposed to fly.

Years passed. And the changeling eagle grew very old. One day, he saw a magnificent bird far above him in the cloudless sky. Hanging with graceful majesty on the powerful wind currents, it soared with scarcely a beat of its strong golden wings.

"What a beautiful bird!" said the changeling eagle to his neighbor. "What is it?"

"That's an eagle—the chief of the birds," the neighbor clucked. "But don't give it a second thought. You could never be like him."

So the changeling eagle never gave it another thought. And it died thinking it was a prairie chicken.[1]

Can you think of anything more tragic than not fulfilling the destiny God has designed for you? For the eagle, that destiny is soaring across the skies. For you and me, it's living above the level of mediocrity.

God has designed you to fly the skies of excellence—not to scratch and peck and grub around on the ground for insects and seeds. It's high time to get your relationship with the Lord off the ground and up in the air. It's time to look up into the heavens—not at the prairie chickens around you. It's time to spread those wings and fly!

To help create a motivational updraft for those outstretched pinions of yours, here are several books we think you will find helpful. Happy flying!

Engstrom, Ted W. *Motivation to Last a Lifetime.* Grand Rapids, Mich.: Zondervan Publishing House, 1984. It's easy to get winded on our quest for excellence—as a result, many give up the quest altogether. What we lack is motivation. In this small but powerful book, Engstrom offers us not just a second wind but resources to keep us going for a lifetime.

1. Ted W. Engstrom, *The Pursuit of Excellence* (Grand Rapids, Mich.: Zondervan Publishing House, 1982), pp. 15–16. Anecdote retold from *What a Day This Can Be,* ed. John Catoir (New York, N.Y.: The Christophers).

————. *The Pursuit of Excellence.* Grand Rapids, Mich.: Zondervan Publishing House, 1982. In this inspiring book, time management expert Ted Engstrom cuts a wide swath through the tall weeds of mediocrity and charts a fresh path toward excellence. Each chapter includes a workable strategy for producing excellence in every area of our lives.

————. *A Time for Commitment.* Grand Rapids, Mich.: Zondervan Publishing House, 1987. Commitment is a sweaty word—it's a *doing* word, not a *feeling* word. This powerful, convicting book will help you roll up your sleeves for a lifetime of commitment and, in doing so, will change the way you view yourself and the world.

————. *Your Gift of Administration: How to Discover and Use It.* Nashville, Tenn.: Thomas Nelson Publishers, 1983. In this helpful book, the author focuses on excellence for the administrator. If you're a leader who has to juggle projects and people, this book will sharpen the personal and professional skills necessary to keep your projects going and your people growing.

Peterson, Eugene H. *Run with the Horses.* Downers Grove, Ill.: InterVarsity Press, 1983. The title comes from Jeremiah 12:5—" 'If you have run with footmen and they have tired you out, / Then how can you compete with horses?' " In a series of profound reflections on the life of Jeremiah, Peterson explores the quest for life at its best and touches the heart of what it means to be fully and genuinely human.

Sanders, J. Oswald. *Spiritual Leadership.* Revised edition. Chicago, Ill.: Moody Press, 1986. A classic for the past twenty years, this book derives its principles for excellence in leadership directly from the Scriptures rather than borrowing them from the world. True spiritual leadership, the author stresses, is authoritative but not authoritarian.

Schaeffer, Franky. *Addicted to Mediocrity: 20th Century Christians and the Arts.* Westchester, Ill.: Crossway Books, 1981. In this *Campus Life* Book of the Year, Schaeffer provocatively demonstrates how Christians today have sacrificed the artistic prominence they enjoyed for centuries and have settled instead for mediocrity. The author offers not only a trenchant critique of Christian commercialism but also some practical direction for recovering the lost gem of artistic excellence.

Stott, John R. W. *The Message of the Sermon on the Mount.* Downers Grove, Ill.: InterVarsity Press, 1978. This excellent exposition of Matthew 5–7 gives the job description for the follower of Christ who wants to live above the level of mediocrity.

Swindoll, Charles R. *Living Above the Level of Mediocrity.* Waco, Tex.: Word Publishing, 1987. Outlining a strategy of commitment to excellence, Swindoll's book will motivate you to get your life off the ground and start flying with the eagles.

White, John. *Excellence in Leadership.* Downers Grove, Ill.: InterVarsity Press, 1986. Using Nehemiah as a model, White confronts the crises Christian leaders face today. Watching Nehemiah overcome his obstacles, we can learn how to hurdle our own.

Notes

Notes

Notes

Notes

Notes

Insight for Living
Cassette Tapes
LIVING ABOVE THE LEVEL OF MEDIOCRITY
A COMMITMENT TO EXCELLENCE

Mediocrity is a rut. It is brown dirt walls of confinement and shovelful after shovelful of sameness. Are you tired of digging that ditch? Are you anxious to break out of the rut? Don't wait any longer. Now is the time to stretch your wings and soar like the eagle God created you to be. These studies in excellence will serve as powerful updrafts to propel your outstretched pinions to new heights . . . to let you glimpse horizons you never knew existed . . . to give you a perspective you never thought possible . . . to help you experience the joy and freedom you scarcely dreamed of, back in the rut of mediocrity.

			U.S.	Canada
LLM	**CS**	**Cassette series—includes album cover**	**$55.25**	**$70.00**
		Individual cassettes—include messages		
		A and B	**5.00**	**6.35**

These prices are effective as of November 1987 and are subject to change without notice.

LLM 1-A: *It Starts in Your Mind (Part One)*—Ephesians 6:11–12; 2 Corinthians 2:11, 10:3–5
     B: *It Starts in Your Mind (Part Two)*—2 Corinthians 10:3–5

LLM 2-A: *It Involves His Kingdom (Part One)*—Romans 14:17, 1 Corinthians 4:20, Daniel 4:4–37
     B: *It Involves His Kingdom (Part Two)*—Luke 19:1–27; Acts 8:10–13, 14:21–22, 19:8–9

LLM 3-A: *It Costs Your Commitment*—Luke 14:25–35
     B: *It Calls for Extravagant Love*—Mark 14:1–9

LLM 4-A: *Vision: Seeing Beyond the Majority*—Numbers 13:25–33, 14:6–9; Matthew 6:31–34
     B: *Determination: Deciding to Hang Tough*—Joshua 14:7–12, 23:6–7, 24:14–15

LLM 5-A: *Priorities: Determining What Comes First*—Matthew 6:33, Colossians 1:13–18, Luke 14:15–35
     B: *Accountability: Answering the Hard Questions*—Romans 14:10–12, Hebrews 13:17, Galatians 6:1–2

LLM 6-A: *Winning the Battle over Greed*—Luke 12:13–34
     B: *Slaying the Dragon of Traditionalism*—Luke 5:27–39

LLM 7-A: *Removing the Blahs from Today*—Psalm 90
     B: *Becoming a Model of Unselfishness*—2 Corinthians 9:6–7, Exodus 35:4–29, 36:2–7

LLM 8-A: *Standing Alone When Outnumbered*—Romans 12:1–2, Deuteronomy 6:10–15
     B: *Standing Tall When Tested*—Judges 3:1–4

LLM 9-A: *Standing Firm When Discouraged*—Judges 6:1–6, 12–16; 7:2–8:35
     B: *Boats, Nets, Fish, and Faith**—Luke 5:1–11

LLM 10-A: *Standing Strong When Tempted (Part One)*—Judges 13:1–16:3
     B: *Standing Strong When Tempted (Part Two)*—Judges 16:4–31

*This message is not a part of the series but is compatible with it.

How to Order by Mail

Ordering is easy and convenient. Simply mark on the order form whether you want the series or individual tapes. Tear out the order form and mail it with your payment to the appropriate address listed under "Ordering Information" at the front of this guide. We will process your order as promptly as we can.

United States orders: If you wish your order to be shipped first-class for faster delivery, please add 10 percent of the total order amount (not including California sales tax). Otherwise, please allow four to six weeks for delivery by fourth-class mail. We accept personal checks, money orders, Visa, and Master-Card in payment for materials. Unfortunately, we are unable to offer invoicing or COD orders.

Canadian orders: Please add 7 percent of your total order for first-class postage and allow approximately four weeks for delivery. For our listeners in British Columbia, a 6 percent sales tax must also be added to the total of all tape orders (not including postage). For further information, please contact our office at (604) 272-5811. We accept personal checks, money orders, Visa, or MasterCard in payment for materials. Unfortunately, we are unable to offer invoicing or COD orders.

Overseas orders: If you live outside the United States or Canada, please allow six to ten weeks for delivery by surface mail. If you would like your order sent airmail, the delivery time may be reduced. Whether you choose surface or airmail delivery, postage costs must be added to the amount of purchase and included with your order. Please use the following chart to determine the correct postage. Due to fluctuating currency rates, we can accept only personal checks made payable in U.S. funds, international money orders, Visa, or MasterCard in payment for materials.

Type of Postage	Cassettes
Surface	10% of total order
Airmail	25% of total order

For Faster Service, Order by Telephone

To purchase using Visa or MasterCard, you are welcome to use our **toll-free** number between the hours of 8:30 A.M. and 4:00 P.M., Pacific time, Monday through Friday. The number is **1-800-772-8888,** and it may be used anywhere in the United States except California, Hawaii, and Alaska. Telephone orders from these states and overseas are handled through our Sales Department at (714) 870-9161. Canadian residents should call (604) 272-5811. We are unable to accept collect calls.

Our Guarantee

Our cassettes are guaranteed for ninety days against faulty performance or breakage due to a defect in the tape. For best results, please be sure your tape recorder is in good operating condition and is cleaned regularly.

Note: To cover processing and handling, there is a $10 fee for *any* returned check.

Order Form

Please send me the following cassette tapes:

The current series: ☐ LLM CS Living Above the Level of Mediocrity

Individual cassettes: ☐ LLM 1 ☐ LLM 2 ☐ LLM 3 ☐ LLM 4
☐ LLM 5 ☐ LLM 6 ☐ LLM 7 ☐ LLM 8
☐ LLM 9 ☐ LLM 10

I am enclosing:

$ _____ To purchase the cassette series for $55.25 (in Canada $70.00*) which includes the album cover

$ _____ To purchase individual tapes at $5.00 each (in Canada $6.35*)

$ _____ Total of purchases

$ _____ If the order will be delivered in California, please add 6 percent sales tax

$ _____ U.S. residents please add 10 percent for first-class shipping and handling if desired

$ _____ *British Columbia residents please add 6 percent sales tax

$ _____ Canadian residents please add 7 percent for postage

$ _____ **Overseas residents please add appropriate postage** (See postage chart under "How to Order by Mail.")

$ _____ As a gift to the Insight for Living radio ministry for which a tax-deductible receipt will be issued

$ _____ **Total amount due (Please do not send cash.)**

Form of payment:

☐ Check or money order made payable to Insight for Living

☐ Credit card (Visa or MasterCard only)

If there is a balance: ☐ apply it as a donation ☐ please refund

---

Credit card purchases:

☐ Visa ☐ MasterCard number _____

Expiration date _____

Signature _____

We cannot process your credit card purchase without your signature.

Name _____

Address _____

_____

City _____

State/Province _____ Zip/Postal code _____

Country _____

Telephone ( ) _____ Radio station __ __ __ __

Should questions arise concerning your order, we may need to contact you.